A CAUSE WORTH LIVING FOR

MY JOURNEY OUT OF TERRORISM

DAVID "PACKIE" HAMILTON

Highland Books

GODALMING
SURREY

First published in 1997 by Highland Books, Two High Pines, Knoll Road, Godalming, Surrey, GU7 2EP. Reprinted 1999

All Scripture quotations, unless otherwise noted, are taken from the New International Version, Copyright © 1973, 1978, 1984 by the International Bible Society. Used by permission of Hodder Headline.

British Library Cataloguing-in-Publication Data. A catalogue record for this book is available from the British Library.

ISBN: 1 897913 42 7

Printed in Great Britain by Caledonian International Book Manufacturing Limited, Glasgow.

PREFACE

Since my release from prison in 1983, I have been asked by many people, "Have you written your story in a book?" When I first prayed about doing so, I felt the Lord laid on my heart to wait for ten years.

It is now 14 years and only because of the continued persistence of a number of people, have I put pen to paper to tell my story. My aim is simple, to glorify the Lord Jesus Christ for his love and mercy toward me, and to show there is no such thing as a hopeless case. If God could break into my life while I was lying in a prison cell, he can reach anyone, anywhere!

I pray God may use this book to reach other "hopeless cases."

David T Hamilton
Manchester 1997

Dedication

This book is dedicated to the three most important women in my life:

My spiritual grandmother, Annie Beggs, who prayed me into the Kingdom of God; to whom I am eternally thankful.

My mother, Christina Hamilton, for her love and devotion to her husband and family for whom her prayers have been unceasing.

My wife Sharon. Of all God's gifts graciously bestowed upon me, she is the one I cherish most, truly a jewel of great price!

CONTENTS

CHAPTER ONE

BORN A PROTESTANT

I was born on a cold, frosty morning in the winter of 1956 in Cookstown, Co. Tyrone.

As the midwife tended to my mother, my father was busy outside in the yard trying to thaw out the pump to draw some water. It was frozen solid, and what little water he got was quickly brought inside and placed on the stove. Even though the delivery went well, there was still much concern. I was six weeks premature, and weighed in at just 3lb 8oz. Quickly bundled up in warm blankets to keep out the bitter cold, I was rushed off to hospital. There I stayed for the next three weeks, and only when I reached the grand weight of 5lb was it deemed safe to allow me home.

The small row of whitewashed cottages is still to be seen today, sunk—it seems—into the ground. These three tiny cottages look really out of place, dwarfed on each side by the more modern looking houses. Only fifteen yards away from the front door now, there is an army road block that checks all vehicles entering the town centre: a constant reminder of the Troubles in Northern Ireland today.

My earliest recollection of childhood was my first day at school. I can recall playing in the sand-pit, and as I looked up I saw my mother's worried face looking through the window of the door. Only when I smiled at her did she turn to walk away, while wiping a tear away from her eye. Perhaps my fondest memory of those early days were my regular visits to my uncle's workshop. He was the town shoemaker. After school, I would run the hundred yards to his workshop, which was situated at the back of the main shop. When I entered through the gate, I was always aware of the smell of the leather. Most times I would find him sitting on a wooden stool, with a boot or shoe held between his knees. He would look up to see who had come in, and as always, he would greet me with a smile.

Usually he would have a mouthful of small nails and a hammer in his hand. I would watch him swing the hammer to his mouth, pick up a single nail and drive it home into the sole of the shoe. As always the nails were in perfect alignment, equally spaced apart. I was always amazed and wondered why he never hit himself with the hammer.

"Can I have a try?" I would ask, but he would just smile and give me a pat on the head, "Maybe when you're older." From that time on I had a desire to work with leather, but little did I know then, where I would later learn my leathercraft; it would be in Belfast gaol!

Like any young family we got up to all kinds of mischief, I remember once my oldest sister, Joy, who was nine years old at the time, decided to make toffee for us when my mother was not at home. She went into the kitchen and poured sugar into a pan and put it on the cooker. I do not know what else she added but whatever it was the toffee tasted nothing like the toffee I would buy in the shop, it was awful. I did not want to eat it, but my big sister insisted I did. My mother arrived home to find me in tears, complaining of a sore tummy.

"It must have been something you've eaten," she said as she rubbed my tummy. I hadn't the nerve to tell her. I knew that look in my big sister's eye, if I dared to tell her I would have been in worse trouble when I went to bed later on!

When I was eight years old, our family moved to another town called Omagh, but I do not have many memories from living there. One year later we moved home again because of my father's work, and this time it was to a large housing estate on the outskirts of Belfast called Rathcoole. Back then it had a population of 14,000 and was believed to be one of the largest housing projects in all of Europe. In our street, which consisted of ten houses, half those were occupied by Roman Catholic families, many of whom were my friends. I can recall playing football together on the field opposite our house. One of the boys playing at that time was called Bobby Sands. Little did any of us know then that we would all be affected by the troubles that were shortly to break out in N. Ireland, that we would be no longer friends, and some of us would even become enemies! Nor did we know then that both Bobby and I, plus quite a few others there, would end up in prison, some as Republican political prisoners and others like me as Loyalists.

Bobby went on to lead the hunger strike protest in the Maze prison, in which he was the first to die. That same night, a Protestant man delivering milk in a Roman Catholic area in Belfast was stoned to death, Both he and his young son, in retaliation for Bobby's death. The irony is that I knew all three of them; they had all come from Rathcoole.

One incident, that I believe was instrumental in discolouring my view of Roman Catholics, happened when I was about nine or ten years of age. I had a Catholic friend called Jim, whose father had a car. Occasionally I would walk down to the Roman Catholic chapel to meet them coming out just to get a ride home in their car. I remember a particular Sunday as I was standing waiting. My friend came out alone. "We have to walk home," he said.

"Why," I asked?

"My father has to go to an IRA meeting," was his reply.

Then it meant nothing to me as I had never heard of the IRA before. But years later that conversation came back to me when I was involved in the tartan gang KAI. I went back to that Catholic chapel again, this time with the gang, around seventy of us, to burn the place down. Only when the police arrived in force and a full-scale riot began, was the chapel saved.

I first became aware of the divide between Protestants and Roman Catholics when I was fourteen years of age. That day I had been skiving off from school and was with a group of other boys, who were all Catholics. We were down in the glen, where amongst the trees we had a swing made from a branch that jutted out over the river. I stood there listening as they began to discuss among themselves what they should do to me. They beat me up and threw me into the river. As I climbed back out of the water, I was still trying to figure out what it was I had done to deserve this beating.

I had to ask them why they did this, and one of them gave me the reason. It was because I was a Protestant and they were all Catholics. Until then I did not know what a Loyalist or a Republican was, or that there was a difference between Protestants and Catholics.

That day was a turning point in my young life, sadly in the wrong direction. I decided never again to have a Catholic friend, only Protestant.

So it was that day when David Hamilton, like so many others among the youth, became a victim of "The Troubles" in Northern Ireland. He was too young then to ever imagine the price he would pay or the consequences he would suffer for making that choice. But back then he thought it was the wisest and safest thing to do.

CHAPTER TWO

RATHCOOLE KAI

Northern Ireland has been embroiled in deadly political fighting for 300 years. There are two separate Irelands. The Republic of Ireland consists of 26 counties. More than 90 percent of its people are Catholic. Northern Ireland is made up of six counties in northeastern Ireland. Most of the inhabitants of the counties, which cover two-thirds of the ancient province of Ulster, are Protestants because of colonisation by England in the seventeenth century. The English confiscated the land of Ulster from local chieftains and divided the acreage among thousands of Protestant English and Scottish settlers who regarded the "native" Irishmen with a mixture of contempt, fear, and desire for their manual labour. The immigration of Protestants into a mostly Catholic land created a lasting division between Protestants and Catholics, and it aggravated the natural conflict between rich and poor and landowners and tenants.

Some Catholics in Northern Ireland still fight for political union with the rest of Ireland. In a united Ireland, Catholics would comprise the vast majority.

For that reason, Protestants in the north continue to resist the reunification of the country.

The bitter division between Protestants and Catholics escalated in this century. After the Easter uprising in Dublin in 1921, Britain recognised the two separate Irelands and armed irregulars of the Irish Republican Army (IRA) threatened raids into the north to force the six counties to join the Republic. Northern Ireland resisted strongly and stepped up efforts to guarantee Protestant rule. The government passed laws that made it legal to arrest people on simple suspicion of belonging to illegal organisations, and laws that established curfews and barred the entry of any undesirable person into the six counties. A heavily armed special part-time police force, called the B Specials, was created to assist the Royal Ulster Constabulary (RUC) in keeping the peace.

Protestants ruled the parliament and controlled every aspect of daily life. They were given preference in jobs and housing. Such inequalities kept alive the spirit of rebellion among Republicans who maintained close ties with the IRA in the south. From the 1930s to the 1950s the IRA carried out sporadic attacks on police barracks and other targets in the north.

A serious assault on Protestant rule of the north came in 1969 after Protestant extremists attacked 500 demonstrators marching from Belfast to Londonderry. IRA recruitment soared as Republicans feared Protestant attacks in all counties. The British government was forced to send 3,000 soldiers to Northern Ireland in July 1969 on a peacekeeping mission. Widespread rioting, brutal raids, and the now-familiar cycle of terrorism, reprisal, and more terrorism took a heavy toll on both civil liberties and lives. The Catholic Nationalists saw the British army as an occupational force, and the IRA was fighting a war on two sides now, not only against the British army but also the Protestant paramilitary organisations that had been born in the conflict.

I was a member of a Tartan gang that was formed in the early 1970s as Protestants armed themselves as vigilantes protecting their own areas from IRA attacks. Street fighting broke out almost every night. Every neighbourhood had its own gang until many of the gangs in Rathcoole combined into a large unit called the Rathcoole KAI. Tragically, the letters K—A—I stood for "Kill All Irishmen."

We were proud to be Ulstermen and proud to be British. We began to terrorise Catholics in the area where we lived. At first we only smashed windows in their houses. Later, we made petrol bombs and set the Catholic school on fire; many homes of Catholics were attacked in this way.

Soon most of the Catholics left Rathcoole for their own safety. We would cheer as we saw families being forced out of their homes. Many Protestants who lived in Catholic areas in the city were also forced out of their homes and moved into Rathcoole to live. My mother cried when our next-door neighbours, a Catholic family, decided to move to an all-Catholic neighbourhood in another part of Belfast.

The same, agressive process took place on mixed estates all over Northern Ireland, as each side wanted supremacy. Soon Rathcoole became known as one of the major Protestant strongholds in the North of Ireland. It is still the same today. Ulster flags fly all the year round. Many walls and footpaths are painted red, white, and blue. Rathcoole was and still is a "no-go" area for Catholics. Workmen entering the area have been murdered just because they were *thought* to be Catholic, when, in fact, they were Protestant. These kinds of killings are carried out by both sides. One girl, whose mother worked with me, told me how her daughter Karen was shot in the throat while leaving her Protestant church. The gunman just wanted to kill a Protestant. When Karen came out of her church he walked up to her, put his arm around her, and said, "I'm going to shoot you." Karen laughed, thinking it was a boy from church playing a joke on her. She died a few weeks later in a hospital.

Sadly, even today these senseless killings continue. Each side is reacting with tit-for-tat murders, so an innocent Protestant or Roman Catholic becomes the next statistic of "The Troubles".

Against this backdrop of murder and fear, I began my teenage years.

Even at school I began to get a name for being crazy when it came to fighting. How this came about was more by accident than anything else, because in fact I acted out of fear rather than temper. Like in all schools we had our share of bullies. One of these guys was a huge skinhead called "Norny". I had seen him on several occasions picking on guys and just roughing them up. A few weeks had passed before he noticed that I was the new kid on the block.

One day I was walking up a narrow corridor on my way to class. The corridor was packed with pupils waiting to go into classrooms as soon as the bell would go to allow them in. Directly in front of me I saw Norny step out. As I passed him by, he immediately jumped unto my back and shouted "Give me a ride!" I was expecting him to do something, so I simply stopped dead and tossed him over my shoulder; he tumbled unto the floor like a sack of coal. Every one started to laugh, accept Norny and me. He started to see red and began to shout what he was going to do to me. I decided not to hang around, and took off down the corridor with Norny close on my heels. There was really nowhere safe to go, so I turned and ran into a classroom. Unfortunately, it was empty. Seconds later Norny came through the door as well. He was pleased to see me standing there alone at the front of the blackboard. As he slowly came towards me I looked a round for something to use as a weapon. Suddenly I saw a wooden blackboard compass and grabbed it. Norny laughed. "What are you going to do with that?" he asked.

I told him "If you lift your hand to hit me I'll stick it in you!"

He laughed again and made a dash toward me. I let him have it straight in his stomach; he gave a scream and fell to the floor clutching his belly. The compass was still embedded in him. There wasn't much blood that I could see, but they took him to hospital anyway. It was the talk of the whole school! I had knifed Norny! And left him for dead in the classroom! At the time I just turned, ran out and went to my class, as if nothing had happened. I honestly wasn't worried by the whole thing: it was his own fault—he asked for it. The Police came in and took me out ten minutes later. (the police station was actually next door to the college). I was cautioned and sent home. Nothing ever came of it. Norny and his bully friends never gave me any bother at school from that day on. He was known as "the bully with two belly buttons" after that!

CHAPTER THREE

UP THE SHANKILL

When the Troubles escalated, vigilantes were formed to protect their own areas, which is how the paramilitaries came into being. One night these men came to talk to the gang leaders; they suggested all the Protestant gangs (there were still a few gangs that had not amalgamated with the other gangs into the KAI) become one as an army, and they would train us as soldiers. That was exactly what we did. For me, this was when my training as a terrorist began; we were issued with army combat clothing, and began to be trained with various weapons.

By this time I had begun to carry a weapon, never going anywhere without a blade. Not that I restricted myself to just using a knife—I'd use anything I could as a weapon. Once when the KAI gang was up in Newcastle on Easter Monday (this was an annual outing for all the Protestant Tartan gangs, who would congregate at this holiday resort), I was sitting in a bar drinking with my girlfriend called Maxine. I got up and went to the toilet; when I returned this guy was sitting up tight beside her trying to kiss her and she struggling to keep him off. As I came back to my seat

I casually asked him if he would like to kiss me. As he was rising up out of his seat, I smashed a pint glass over his head and left him lying in a cocktail of blood and beer. Suddenly one of his mates hit me on the back of the head from behind and knocked me into a stack of beer crates. As I got up I grabbed a bottle and when he ran at me I smashed it over his head. I was still holding the neck of the broken bottle in my hand when a third guy attacked me from the side. I turned and caught him by the back of his hair and plunged the bottle neck up into his face. I heard him scream and when I looked at him his nose was gone! A fourth man started to approach me, but when he saw the state of his friend's face he soon changed his mind, and shaking his hands and head he began to back off.

I was saturated with blood all down the front of me. I ran out of the lounge and into another part of the bar. I saw someone I knew and he took off a large woollen jumper and I put it over my tee-shirt. A few moments later, the police rushed in; they stood in the middle of the floor, "Can you see him here?" one of them asked.

This guy looked around the crowded in the room, when he saw me his eyes stopped, He stared at me, I just stared back at him—it was the same man that had backed off moments earlier. He then said "No I don't see him." They turned and went out again. The bartender also knew it was me but decided it was in his own best interests to stay quiet, I have never stepped foot in that bar since that day, yet 12 years later in Belfast I was talking to a stranger who reminded me of this incident—it turned out he was the bartender in question. I asked him how he had remembered the incident and how he knew I was the one involved. His answer: "it's not every day you see someone having their nose cut off, is it?"

Because the Police were watching the gang members in our area, obviously we all became well known to them. So I decided to join a paramilitary unit outside my neighbourhood, something I would later regret. It was a team on the Shankill Road, a famous area in Belfast that is seen by Loyalists everywhere as the heart of Ulster Protestantism.

It was during my time "up the Shankill" that I was shot.

Often I stayed up the Shankill road for three or four days without going home. The night I got shot I was in a house that gang members often stayed in. A fellow member was ordered to do a knee-capping (this meant punishing petty thieves or consistent joy riders by shooting them in the area of the knee, sometimes both knees, depending on the seriousness of their crime) He asked me to go along with him. Ten minutes later we were standing on a street corner. My job was to watch out for the Security Forces. As I turned around to ask him who the target was to be, he answered, "You!" and lifted the gun up to the side of my head. I immediately reached up and grabbed his arm which held the gun. As I pulled his hand down, the gun went off. I heard three very loud bangs and for a moment I thought I was deaf. All I could hear was the ringing in my ears. I started running and felt a burning sensation in my foot and leg. I stopped to look but could see nothing wrong. But when I kicked my shoe off I saw blood everywhere. I was bleeding in three different places. I could not put my foot back down on the ground and stood holding on to a lamp post. Some neighbours came out to investigate the shots. They carried me into a club across the street and laid me on a pool table.

After a few minutes a stranger arrived and examined me. He spoke authoritatively, "He needs to go the hospital or he could bleed to death. He has possibly three bullets in him." The man quickly put me in a car and took me to a hospital that thankfully was only a few miles away. He carried me into the hospital over his shoulder and laid me on a stretcher. "This young lad has been shot," he said, and turned around and walked out.

The police soon arrived to question me about my gunshot wounds. The officer asked me my name and where I lived. "Why do you need my name?" I asked. The grumpy officer said, "We need to inform your parents and get their permission to operate." I was concerned about my mother who had a heart condition. I thought, "If she hears I've been shot, she surely will have a heart attack." The officer tried to reassure me that they had ways of breaking such news to people but I wasn't convinced. He then became annoyed with me and began to shout, "Listen to me, boy, I want your name and I want it right now. Otherwise, you're in big trouble."

"OK," I said, "My name is Francis McFrancis."

The policeman left to talk to the hospital staff. I decided it was also time for me to leave. I got up and hopped across the room and cautiously opened the door just enough to peer out at the corridor to see if any other police were around. The way seemed clear and I hopped along the corridor and breathed a sigh of relief as I made it around the corner. "Almost free,"

I thought. The next thing I heard was the sound of heavy boots running down the corridor.

"Where do one think you're going?" the voice of my friendly policeman boomed. I knew he was glad to see me because he led me back to my little room and placed a guard outside to keep me company.

Some of my friends came to see me the next day. When they tried to slip into my room, the policeman asked them, "And where do you lot think you are going to?" They replied, "We're here to see a patient." He asked, "And who might that be?" one of my friends shouted back, "Packie Hamilton."

"OK, thank you," he said, as he wrote my identity down in his little black book.

I remember coming out of the operating room on a trolley. As I passed through the swinging doors I looked up and there were my parents standing there. I shall never forget the anguish on my mother's face. My father had his arm around her shoulder, trying to console her. When I saw her I began to cry too. I showed her the two bullets that the doctor let me keep. Today I carry the third bullet still in my foot. The doctor thought it would do more damage to remove the bullet than to allow it to remain in my foot. It is a constant reminder to me that bullets can kill. I also learned it was safer to stay in one's own area—the Organisation didn't trust me, it seems, because I didn't join a team in my own area; they decided to kill me in case I was 'a plant' trying to infiltrate their ranks. 'Don't trust anyone' was the motto of the day, and they were taking no chances.

Today I am still known by many in Ireland as "Packie", in fact many of my friends in the South of Ireland would not even know what my proper name is.

"Packie" is Irish for Patrick, but that is not the reason I got called it, rather it was because in the summer I would go a very deep brown. One day one of my mates called Alfie said "David looks like a Pakistani! we should call him Packie from now on." Of course all the boys were laughing, and so the name stuck.

In the early seventies, there was much rioting on the streets of Northern Ireland. Rathcoole had its share of it. Once during a riot we attacked an army patrol and tried to steal the weapon off a soldier as he lay on the ground. The gun was attached to his wrist by a strap. We were unable to detach it but grabbed the magazine from out of the weapon and ran away to avoid being captured.

One night I had been on sentry duty outside the club (we had a security rota to stop the place from being bombed). I slept late the next morning but as I woke up in bed I knew I would be in big trouble if I didn't get the gun back to the place where most of our weapons were kept. I got dressed and put the gun down the waistband of my trousers. I pulled on a denim jacket before going down stairs and checked in the mirror to make sure the gun could not be seen. Memories were fresh in my mind about an incident a month before when I had brought a gun into the house. I had been so sure that even if the police raided our house again they would never find the gun. Much to my surprise my mother found it and went berserk. She was shouting and crying at the same time. She said if I ever killed anyone it would be her death too.

I argued back. "We are at war with the IRA. Someone has to fight them! The police and army are restrained because of red tape. Their hands are tied."

"I don't care," she replied, "Murder is murder no matter what. I could not live with the knowledge that one had killed someone's son and left a mother or a young wife and family mourning."

That was not the end of my problems over bringing a gun into the house. When my father got home and found out, he called me into the front room. When I closed the door and turned around he punched me hard. He grabbed me by the throat, shoved me up against the wall, put his face close to mine and yelled, "As long as you live, never bring another gun into this house." All I could do was nod my head. From then on I made sure that whenever I carried a gun, I did not bring it home. I knew my old man was serious. When he said something he only said it once. He would have beaten me to a pulp even though I was 17 and loved fighting.

My dad was the toughest man I knew. He had boxed at the highest level in the British Army. Because he was excellent with a skipping rope they nicknamed him "The Skipper." Even now that he is older, I still would not want to cross him. Years later the police were interrogating me at the police holding centre in Ladus Drive, Belfast, when the detective found out who my father was. He sat back in his chair—I could see he was afraid now—and immediately turned around and told the other officer sitting beside him not to lay a hand on me. (It was common in those days to receive a beating while in police custody.) The detective went on to say my father would kill him if he thought he had so much as laid a finger on me while questioning me. He told his partner stories about how tough my father was. I just sat there and smiled. I was proud to be Cecil Hamilton's son.

There were times I did things on the spur of the moment. Once I was walking with my wife and pushing my child in a pram. We met a large number of young gang members, who were not old enough to join the ranks of the paramilitary group. I asked them what they were up to and one of them told me they planned to stone a bus in retaliation for police harassment earlier. I told them to wait and I would hijack a bus for them to burn. I turned to my wife and said "I'll see you later." Before she could answer, I had run off with them. I told them to hide when I saw a bus coming. The plan was I would board the bus and order every one off except the driver, who could drive the bus for us. When the bus stopped, I gave the signal and they all came out from hiding and boarded the bus. We drove it up into Rathcoole, set it across the main road and torched it. I left them to it and went back up to meet my wife at the shops again, as if nothing had happened. I didn't care less about getting caught for it. Maxine didn't mention it; neither did I.

One morning as I walked through the estate to the Diamond shopping centre I saw two of my friends standing outside a shop. I crossed the square and walked into the shop behind them. As I stood at the door waiting, the shopkeeper looked past my friends and stared at me. I saw fear spread across his face as he looked down at my waist. I realised the handle of my gun was protruding from under my jacket. He shouted at the top of his voice, "Don't shoot, don't shoot!" I didn't know what to do so I turned and ran out of the door. My friends followed and we ran across the square. A few minutes later we sat and talked about what had happened. We thought it was funny. None of us knew just how serious it was. Little did we know we would all end up in prison charged with attempted armed robbery!

When I arrived at home that night a heavily armoured police Land Rover was pulling away from my house. Some of the neighbours stood at their gates gossiping, asking what the police were doing at the Hamilton house. I made myself scarce. When it got dark I went home. My dad met me at the door and told me the police had been looking for me. I told dad what had really happened and that my friends and I had decided to go to Scotland until things cooled down.

A few hours later my friend Albert and I stole a car and drove to Larne harbour to catch the ferry. We had gone only a few miles when we heard a police siren. I looked out the rear window and saw the familiar police vehicle. "Hold on," I shouted and pushed the accelerator to the floor. The police Land Rover, weighted down with armour, was no match for our stolen car. This was my first police chase!

It felt pretty good to escape the clutches of the police who were looking for us. We got onto country roads and widened the gap between the police and us. It was obvious that the police had given up hope of catching us, or so I thought.

We sat in a dark farm lane and laughed at how easily it had been to give the police the slip. After a while we thought it was safe to go catch the ferry. Albert wanted to drive and took the wheel. We had driven only three miles when we rounded the bend—straight into a police road block.

"We're caught Packie!" he screamed.

"Not yet," I replied. "Drive up the grass bank and go around them. There's enough room to pass."

As the car mounted the curb the police officers jumped out of the way.

"We're going to make it, Albert!" I yelled.

Albert was not the world's best driver and swerved all over the road. He lost control and the car veered into a wall on the opposite side of the road and came to a grinding halt. We were only about 300 metres from the police.

"Run Albert!" I shouted. We ran across the back gardens of the nearby homes. I could hear our pursuers close behind.

I jumped into a lily pond to hide. I peered out from the lilies just as policemen with torches ran by. I climbed out of the pond a few minutes later and looked for Albert. When I quietly called out his name his head popped up from inside a rubbish bin.

We confidently walked down the street until a car suddenly screeched to a halt. "Like a lift boys?" It was the police and we were caught!

We were put into separate cells at the police station so we could not compare stories. I thought I was hearing things when the officer said Albert and I could not leave unless we confessed to stealing the car. I realised this police station was not aware of the attempted armed robbery charge we were expecting. Albert and I quickly confessed to stealing the car!

We were excited about our unexpected release and were amazed at our luck that no detectives were in the station at the time of our arrest. Otherwise we would have been charged and jailed to await our trial.

Shortly we were on board the ferry heading for Scotland. We stayed almost six months in Glasgow, drinking and partying, and going to Rangers and Celtic football matches. One day I received a letter from my mother telling me that my oldest sister was getting married in a few weeks. I decided to go home for the wedding even though I knew the police were looking for me for other crimes, including a petrol bombing of what we believed was an army post for gathering intelligence. We were almost killed because the bomb we ourselves had planted exploded while we were still in the building. The guy with me was badly burned. I had heard whilst in Scotland that he was in prison awaiting trial for the bombing. This did not put me off from going home; I wasn't going to miss my sister's wedding! Albert decided to come home as well.

Boarding the ship, we decided to get a comfortable seat down in the lounge. The crossing would take almost four hours, so I planned to sleep for a few hours. Albert played the fruit machines and ended up penniless. As I was ordering a drink, I saw a young woman in the queue with her back to me. I could not believe my eyes, it was my younger sister Beth! She was thrilled to see me, so we sat and talked throughout the whole trip. This made it seem a lot shorter. I was surprised to learn my mother and father were planning to pick her up after we docked. She told me she had been over in Scotland for a holiday. I can still see the joy on my parents' faces at the ferry port as they saw us both coming down the gang plank. It was a time of great reunion for us all.

My sister's wedding went off really well. Everyone had a great time and were waiting to send Joy and her husband off on their honeymoon. Joy began to cry because she thought surely the police would catch me and send me to gaol. She suddenly decided that I should go with them on their honeymoon. I just laughed and refused the offer —much to the relief of her new husband.

I noticed two strangers standing across the street from the church. Every time I looked at them, they looked away. I had my suspicions. I deliberately allowed them to see me. I knew I was far enough away that I could easily escape if they chased me. I excused myself and told my sister I wanted to go around behind the church for a smoke. When the men saw me leaving they started running across the street. As soon as I was out of sight I climbed over the hedge surrounding the church. I looked back and saw two faces peeping around the corner of the church. I gave the two plain clothes detectives a friendly wave and was gone.

The next day I was not so quick. As I walked up to my girlfriend's house, two police officers appeared from nowhere. They each grabbed an arm and walked me down the path to an unmarked car.

I called out to Maxine my girlfriend, "Don't worry, I'll be back shortly."

One of the policeman said, "Yeah, don't hold your breath waiting."

I didn't know it then but it would be eight months before I would be back again. Eight months, the length of my first stay in Her Majesty's Prison.

CHAPTER FOUR

BEHIND THE WIRE

The ride to gaol I will never forget! Albert had already been arrested and we were hand-cuffed together in the back seat. At first we thought it was funny pulling each other's arm with the handcuffs. The fun wore off quickly and we became very quiet. The sombreness of where we were heading landed like a ton of bricks on our shoulders. I realised it might be a long time before I would see Rathcoole again so I made sure I had a good look out of the window to have something to remember.

As the car stopped at the prison gate I looked up at the huge stone grey walls. It was strange how I saw them in a different way that day. I was not up to visit this time. No, this time I was here to stay!

A few moments later the huge double gates swung open to allow us access. The sound of the steel gates closing behind us echoed in my ears. It sounded like thunder. We sat in the darkness and a cold shudder ran down my spine. I thought, "This is prison. It's not television. This is for real."

I heard another heavy rumbling sound as the gates in front of us opened, letting light pour into the tunnel. The car drove slowly across the courtyard and stopped at a sign that read "Reception".

We were led into the reception area and put into separate wooden cubicles for processing.

As I sat there wondering what would happen next, I listened to all the noise. It seemed ages before the bolt on my door was pulled back and an officer with a dark blue overall coat ordered me out. He told me to follow him over to a counter, where he began to write down all my particulars. Afterwards he told an orderly to take us through for a bath. There were other orderlies working there, their uniforms consisted of a blue and white thin-striped shirt and a pair of grey denim trousers.

I noticed one of them had a denim waistcoat on. I found out later on this guy was a long-term prisoner and the other two were short-term prisoners. All the long-term men wore their uniforms tailored to suit themselves, whereas short-term men had to wear whatever they were given to wear. None of them were privileged to wear a waistcoat.

The bathhouse consisted of three cells, 8' x 12', each with a half stable-door. Inside was a huge cast iron tub, which had lost its white enamel a century before. I searched in vain for a plug, all I could see was a piece of wood carved out to fit the plug hole. It must have been there a long time because it was well worn, smoothed over the years of constant use. A few moments later I was happy to hear my friend's voice.

I called out to him, "Albert don't forget to wash behind your ears!" His head appeared over the stable door, "Looks like your bathroom at home," he called out as he went back for his bath next door.

I could hear him trying to sing next door, it seemed to echo around the place. A few minutes later the orderly appeared with a blue towel which he tossed over the door. He set down on the floor a toothbrush, soap, and a large plastic mug that had a grey knife, fork and spoon in it. After getting dried and dressed again I lifted the mug to examine it, it was disgusting. It had been white many years ago, but was now a dirty cream colour. The inside was worse, it was stained dark brown from the gaol tea. Some prisoner had started to carve out his name, it seemed, on the base but had not finished the task. The letters looked crude, hacked out with a razor blade. There was a bottle of bleach up on the window ledge used to clean the bath, so I poured some into my cup. There was an immediate change, the bleach seemed to climb up the inside of the cup. I began to wash the outside of the cup as well. In two minutes, apart from the carvings, you would have thought it was a new mug. I rinsed it off under the hot tap and it was ready for use.

We were put in a cell together for the night. The walls were painted pink. Seemed very homely!

There was a window about eight feet off the ground, if you stood on top of the frame of the iron bed it was possible to pull yourself up by the window bars to look out—not that there was much to see.

I lay down on my bed listening to all the strange noises. It seemed doors were being opened and closed afar off somewhere, there was also the rattling of keys.

As I lay there, I realised that the noise of the doors opening was coming closer to us.

Five minutes later the keys turned in our door, and an orderly stood with a steel bucket. "Do ya want tay? Dip your cup in."

Another orderly was holding a tray bake; he handed us two bits of square cake, covered in red jam and coconut flake: " Enjoy your supper lads." Before I got a chance to answer, the door banged shut again.

I looked at this strange coloured liquid in my mug. Was it tea, coffee or Guinness, a mixture of all three perhaps? It seemed very strong, with the essence of milk. I looked over at Albert; he was staring into the cup as well. When he looked up both of us began to laugh. Albert mused, "So this is gaol. We'd better get used to this stuff."

As the night wore on, we listened to conversations going on around us, as other prisoners shouted out through the bars to each other. Eventually things quieted down The naked light-bulb began to flicker. I heard the sound of footsteps coming closer along the landing. The officer or "screw" (slang for prison officer, because the old handcuffs used in prisons did not use keys, instead they worked by a screw mechanism) was walking along the landing turning out the lights. The lights were turned out at eleven o'clock each night. Our door flap lifted briefly, and I caught a glimpse of a pair of eyes before we were left totally in the darkness. After our eyes grew accustomed to the dark I just lay and stared at the cell wall, looking at the irregular rectangular shapes formed by the shadow of the iron bars as the moonlight shone through into our cell.

Eventually we went to sleep.

The next morning we were awakened early by the screw and told to "slop-out"—that means to go and empty your chamber-pot (there were no toilets in the cell then, like they have today). Each man had his own pot. You queued up at the slop house to wash and empty your pot out; the smell of urine hung heavy in the air throughout the prison.

Later on that morning we were moved over to C Wing, which was for Loyalist prisoners only. After meeting the wing leaders we were accepted and allowed to stay.

We had been in gaol just a few weeks when a prison officer outside was murdered by the IRA. The authorities cancelled all prison visits the following day and we were locked in our cells (at that time we were entitled to three visits a week because we were on remand and not yet sentenced). When we were released for supper the leaders decided to riot in protest. Quickly a plan was devised to take over the wing and capture some of the guards. When the signal was given, men attacked the few guards who were standing around. Next thing I knew everyone started wrecking the place. Chairs were smashed, table legs were broken off and used as weapons. Prisoners built barricades to prevent the riot squad from coming into the wing.

Alarm bells were continuously ringing. Prisoners were running all over the place arming themselves with all kinds of weapons.

For the next few days prison authorities tried unsuccessfully to regain control of the wing. Finally in desperation they called in the army. The soldiers smashed their way in through the roof and attacked every prisoner in sight. It was fierce hand-to-hand fighting. It didn't take them long to overpower us, having double the manpower and firing rubber bullets; we knew we didn't stand a chance.

Some guys locked themselves in cells to try to avoid getting shot or beaten by the soldiers and screws. Afterwards we were stripped naked and handcuffed to the hot water pipe that ran beneath the window just three inches off the floor. Most of the cell doors were broken so the only way they could keep us contained was to handcuff us to the pipe. There we stayed for the next three days until all the doors had been replaced. There was nothing left in our cells. Beds and doors had been piled up as barricades. Clothing was scattered everywhere on the safety wire between the landings.

A few days later I had to make an appearance at court. When I was told to get dressed I asked what clothes I was to wear: "Whatever you find out there. Go and find something to put on."

I spent an hour searching in the rubble for something to wear. I knew not to ask for an iron! It was weeks before tensions settled and we were allowed back out of our cells again. I did not know it then, but I would relive this episode a few years later.

After six months I finally was informed in writing what I was charged with. The usual routine was to be moved down to another prison called Long Kesh to await trial. No one liked the trip to Long Kesh. We were put into a vehicle similar to a horse box. We were handcuffed and locked in a cubicle no larger than a dressing-room locker. When you sat down your knees were under the seat of the man in front of you. When the door was shut it was hard not to feel claustrophobic. I heard other men begin to panic as they screamed for their doors to be opened. The guards told them to shut up and be quiet.

When I knew I would be going down, the night before I would try to stay awake reading (by moonlight) and then when my journey started, hopefully, I would doze off. You could never fall fast asleep, the sway of the truck would stop you. But you could sort of doze a little. Doing this made the journey seem shorter.

Long Kesh was an old air base from World War II. It was made up of a dozen compounds. The first six consisted of prisoners who were interned.

These were all men the security forces suspected of being members of paramilitary groups. They were arrested and put in gaol without any trial, neither did they have a release date of any sort.

Some of these men were held for a long time like this. They were known as "the Internees" At least other prisoners had a release date, but not these; they were in limbo!

Because political status was still in force at that time (it was done away with three years later, in 1976), Long Kesh was run as a training school for Terrorists.

We even wore our own uniforms! Each morning we all gathered in the exercise yard and had to do parade drill. Afterwards we would do weapon training! Sounds incredible but it's the truth; we even had bomb-making lessons!

Each compound was made up of four army billet huts made of corrugated iron that the prisoners slept in. There was another hut used for the toilets and the whole place was surrounded by a galvanised wire fence, about six metres high.

On the top of the fence was razor wire, a typical prisoner-of-war camp. It was possible to see through the wire into the next compound, which was full of Republican prisoners. The authorities thought doing this would stop communication between other Loyalist compounds. They assumed because we were enemies we would not bother with each other.

It didn't work. If we wanted a message passed down to another of the Protestant compounds we would shout over to the Republicans and then throw the message attached to a half-pound block of butter (prison ration) over to them, and they would then in turn throw it over to the next compound. You could stand and watch to make sure they passed it on.

It was an unspoken rule, you did not interfere with any of these notes you simply passed them on. So each group could keep in touch with their own kind in any of the other compounds.

I was put in compound nine, for the remands (those awaiting trial), and this was my home for the next few months. I remember one of my first prison visits at that time was from my mother and the girl next door; her name was Sharon—I thought she was beautiful. I remember the first time I set eyes on her, my family having not long moved to Belfast: one day I was walking up the garden path which we shared and she was standing with her mum at the front door talking to my mum. It made my day when I found out she was my neighbour! When I joined the Tartan gang, she it was who sewed the tartan on my denim jacket. I tried once to get a kiss from her when she was in our house, I was only fifteen at the time. I tried to grab her but she pulled away and ran out the back door. I gave up chasing her, thinking she wasn't interested in me as a boyfriend. She was the girl who visited me when I was in gaol for the first time, and as God would have it, she would be the woman who would be waiting for me at the gate when I left gaol for the last time, ten years later—but a lot of things would happen to both of us before we would be joined together in matrimony

It was very near Christmas and the courts would soon close. So I knew it would be early in the new year (1974) before my trial would come to court. I just tried to settle down and wait. Let the time pass.

Life in Long Kesh was a little better than the Crumlin Road jail. For one thing we had less contact with the screws. We were locked in a wire compound and the screws stayed on the outside. That suited us fine, because it meant we could do whatever we wanted.

We looked forward to the weekends; they were more slack—we didn't parade or have classes. On Saturday nights we had a sing-along and made home-brew to drink. The home-brew was more like rocket fuel than a drink. It was made of a mixture of fruit and petrol from our cigarette lighters. Sometimes we threw in brass and copper polish to add to the taste. I was always amazed how the colour and taste were never the name.

Perhaps my worst experience in prison was on Christmas day, 1973. We had drunk home-brew all day. Later on in the evening my friend Geordie and I were lying on the bed watching television when he asked me if I would smuggle some cigarettes up to the kitchen for his brother who worked there. I said no problem and promised I would make a trip to the kitchen the next morning. Later on that night, we heard someone screaming and a few minutes later everything went strangely quiet. The following morning we were wakened by the sound of the sirens going off. Apparently when the screws came to unlock the hut doors, they found a battered body lying in a pool of blood.

It was that of my friend Geordie! We were locked up for two weeks while the authorities tried to solve the murder. Like most prison murders no one was ever charged for it. When we finally were unlocked, we all went in next door.

I shall never forget the sick feeling I had when I saw the pool of blood. We didn't expect to see that. The authorities just left it the way they had found it, it hadn't been touched, never mind cleaned up. I had seen plenty of blood in my time—the scars on my arms and hands are vivid reminders that violence played a big part in my life—but this was altogether different. Everyone just stared at the large dark red stain of congealed blood in the middle of the floor. I don't think anyone spoke; if they did, I wasn't aware of it. No one wanted to go near it. After a few minutes I told them I would wash it off. After all, he had been one of my mates.

Geordie's murder had a profound affect on a lot of people. Many of the guys, including me, lost the desire for the home-brew after that.

CHAPTER FIVE

UP FOR TRIAL

Shortly after that I was moved back up to the Crumlin Road gaol, which meant my trial would be pretty soon. It was around this time I began to pray again (I had not prayed since I was a young boy). Not that they were long prayers, mostly one-liners like "God get me out of here and I'll be good from now on". I had learned about God at Sunday school; I believed God existed OK and thought if I make a deal with him he will help me beat this rap. So I began to pray every day when it would enter my mind.

Other days I prayed something like, "God I promise I'll start going back to church again if you just get me out!". I thought that was a good deal, if I prayed it once, I must have prayed it a hundred times.

When my trial came up eventually, the judge sentenced me to a five-year stretch. I couldn't believe it! For an attempted armed robbery and stealing a few cars! To me it was no robbery, it was more of a joke. Only now it was far from being funny: who said praying helps? It didn't seem to help me!

That night as I lay in my cell looking up at the ceiling. I thought, *five years! that's what happens when you pray.*

I was sick at the thought, until I noticed someone had written their name up in the corner of the wall. As I stared up at it I was shocked to see whose name it was. It was the name of my friend who had been murdered a few months before. I couldn't believe it, neither could I grumble; it stopped me feeling sorry for myself.

At least I was alive.

I didn't even bother to undress that night, I lay down on top of the bed. It was well into the early hours of the morning before I finally got to sleep. It was the screw who woke me up as he banged up the door, i.e. locking it back to the wall.

As I looked out at him he said, "Get ready for court Hamilton."

"Not me," I shouted back.

"Listen Hamilton, I've orders to get you over to the court, so get washed right now you are going, like it or not."

The High Court in Northern Ireland is only across the road from the prison in Belfast. In fact, you do not even have to leave the prison to go to court. The two buildings are connected by an underground tunnel that runs beneath the main road. Walking through the tunnel was unpleasant, to say the least. It was very hot and clammy. From the moment you begin the six minute walk across you are aware of the lack of air down there. There are huge water pipes that run the length of the tunnel along one side that are caged off, in case someone should get burnt accidentally.

After climbing up the steps at the other end I passed through the door, and suddenly found myself standing in the dock of a courtroom with a prison officer on each side of me. I was amazed to find the place was empty apart from the two prison officers and myself.

I did not really know what to expect in court; as far as I was aware all four of my charges where dealt with the day before. I was worried in case I got more time added on to my existing five years. As I stood there in the dock with all kinds of thoughts racing through my mind, a door across the room opened and I saw a familiar face; it was my barrister. At last I'll get some answers, he will know what this is all about, or so I thought. "What are the charges against me today?" I asked, I could not believe it when he turned his hands up and shrugged his shoulders, saying he did not know either!

Like me, he also had been strangely summoned to the courtroom that morning as well. I was really discouraged then. How could my lawyer provide a defence for me if he didn't even know what charges were being brought? Things looked bad. I began to sweat. Before I got a chance to challenge him, two officers came through from the judge's chamber.

"Everyone please stand," the bailiff bellowed as the judge entered the courtroom.

We then took our seats again. I began to study the judge, hoping he was in a good mood today. He looked very solemn sitting there with all his long robes on and the traditional white wig perched on his head. It's amazing what enters your mind at times. I was trying to figure out what kept his spectacles on the end of his nose. Occasionally he would lower his head to peep over the rim at me—I was waiting for them to fall off. It's a good thing they did not, or I would have gone into a fit of laughter and ended up with more time for contempt of court.

I had to stand up the whole time while the judge was speaking to me. To be perfectly honest, I was not really paying much attention to the lecture he was giving me. Occasionally I nodded my head towards him to give the impression that I was paying attention. But when I heard him say that he had decided to change my sentence to a recorded sentence, (a recorded sentence is when the offender is released and his custodial sentence is only implemented if he reoffends), I could not believe my ears! As I was looking around in amazement, I saw my mother sitting in the public gallery. I gave her a huge smile and the thumbs up sign, I was going home! A free man! Perhaps there was something in this prayer business after all.

The judge went on to say he did not want to see my face ever again. Sad to say we were to meet again, not that long after. Not only that, but he would remember my face as well.

A few months later, I was sitting in a restaurant along with my girlfriend Maxine (I started to date her again when I came home from prison) and another couple. Although we had been drinking all evening I could not seem to get drunk. I was aware that the place where we were eating was not a safe place for any Protestant to be because it was adjacent to a strong

Republican neighbourhood. I was glad when we paid the bill and headed toward the door.

As we left the restaurant I saw two men standing a few yards away, one of them was bent over appearing to be sick, the other man had his arm across his friends back. I thought it was strange because the man standing up never took his eyes off me the whole time as we were passing by. All at once the man who was bent over straightened up and pulled a gun from under his jacket! I shouted to my friends, "Run, he has a gun". I did not know which way to run. In front of me, across the road was an open field, it was pitch black over there. I decided to make a dash there, but suddenly stopped turned around and ran back into the restaurant. I was puzzled with my own behaviour; it seemed silly to run back into the restaurant. Inside the door I shouted a warning. No one moved: they all just sat and stared at me. I heard the door being kicked open and looked around to see one of the gunmen coming in. I began to run again, knocking tables over as I made my way through the kitchen. I could see the startled faces of the Chinese cooks, who knew by my face that something was seriously wrong. I just managed to get the back door open when I heard the gunman behind me run into the kitchen. I jumped on to a pile of rubbish bins and leapt on to the top of the wall, knowing the gunman was not far behind me. Just as I dropped down into the alley I heard the large crack of two shots. As soon as my feet touched the ground I was away. It was not safe yet; these guys knew the area as well as I did, if not better. I ran up onto the railway tracks, which ran along by the beach. I cursed the moon. It was shining bright, too bright. "What a beautiful night to be murdered."

I was silhouetted against the night sky, thanks to the moon! Suddenly the deadly silence was shattered by the sound of more gunfire. I immediately threw myself down to the ground for cover behind the railway lines. Other shots followed, but they were different from the others, which made me think something else was happening now, the next thing I heard was the sirens of the security forces piercing the night air, as they arrived on the scene. It was only then that I knew it was safe to return to the restaurant. As I was walking back, I was worried about how Maxine and my two friends had fared. As I got back, the place was swarming with security forces. It seemed the police saw one of the gunmen and started to give chase, but they ran into the field and were able to escape being captured. I found out later they had knocked Maxine to the ground, as they started to chase after me. Although shaken up both she and my friends were safe and sound. Their faces said it all. They had heard the shots and were afraid I was lying dead or seriously wounded somewhere. The police officer came over to us and asked me how did I know to turn back. He went on to tell me there had been a gunman waiting across the road in the field. My attackers had expected me to run there for cover because it was the most obvious place to go. For no apparent reason I had turned back again to the restaurant.

Had I continued running, I surely would have been killed at point-blank range! Every one said I was extremely lucky, I had narrowly escaped death. But I just laughed. I was too smart for them boys!

It would be years before I would know the truth that it was God who made me turn and run in the other direction. It was God who spared my life. But for the time being, I carried on with my usual crazy life style. Nothing changed apart from one thing; I made sure I avoided that particular restaurant. Since then, I have never been comfortable sitting with my back to the door in any restaurant.

My dad sincerely wanted me to work hard and stay out of trouble and prison. Although only out of prison that Friday morning, before taking me home he drove me up to the factory where I had been serving my apprenticeship as a welder before going to prison. The manager kindly gave me my job back, so the following Monday I was back at work! I didn't share my dad's enthusiasm about working but he thought my job would keep me out of paramilitary organisations. Sadly it didn't work. I wasn't out that long before I joined the organisation again—in fact it was the following night.

I had felt peer pressure from my mates to get back involved in the Troubles. Almost everyone my age was a member of one terrorist groups or another. If you were not involved, you were a "nobody" and had no protection from any of the gangs that controlled the neighbourhoods. I had already decided to join another group called the Ulster Volunteer Force. The UVF was more militant and violent against the IRA; they were also very secretive. I was intrigued by them. The only way to join the UVF was by invitation from one of its present members. I had made it known around the gaol that I wanted to join. I didn't have long to wait before two strangers came to my home and asked if I wanted to be part of their group. I said yes. They gave me a week to think it over because they told me once you're in the UVF, you're in for life.

A week later the men showed up at my house again. When I told them I definitely wanted to join they told me to go to a bar nearby.

I remember walking through the doorway into the public bar, I didn't know what to expect. It was dimly lit and the smell of stale alcohol hung heavy in the air. Only a few of the old regulars were to be seen, huddled together in the corner. Above their heads a television blared away, forcing them to shout to be heard. None of them had the wit to turn the thing down or off.

I nodded to the barman who was busy drying beer glasses behind the counter. He nodded toward the other door, telling me where I was to go. I entered the door and a man stepped in front of me and put his finger on my chest.

"Are you sure you want to do this?" he asked. "This is your last chance to say no. After this there can be no turning back."

"Yes, I want to," I replied. "This is a cause worth dying for."

That afternoon I took the oath of loyalty and became a member of the Ulster Volunteer Force. As I left the pub I thought to myself, "Only God knows what the future holds for me." All I was sure of was that things would never be the same from that day on.

Shortly after I had joined we planned a bank robbery. I was annoyed because they planned the heist for Thursday morning. That was the day I had to pick up my paycheque so I couldn't take part in the robbery.

When I came home from work that night my mate's wife was crying. She told me her husband had not come home. We watched the local television news and discovered four men, one of them her husband, had been arrested during a bank robbery earlier that day. Even though my best friend was in gaol, it did nothing to deter me, I still carried on.

Maxine, my girlfriend became pregnant and we decided to get married. She knew that I was involved in the UVF and pleaded with me to try to find a way to get out. To keep her quiet I promised I would. But I lied.

Our son was born a few months after we were married. I went up to see my newborn son on the night he was born. I wasn't all that keen to visit the hospital it was situated in a Republican area in Belfast, not a safe place for any Protestant to walk through. I was wearing my good suit (my wedding suit, kept for wedding and funerals). I also had a bunch of flowers with me and something else. I knew I had to walk through an army checkpoint, but decided to take the risk anyway. Passing through the barrier I raised my arms up to allow the soldier to frisk me. I was watching his face, and saw his expression change when he felt something down the back of my trousers.

"What's this for?" the soldier asked. Pulling a large kitchen knife out from under my coat. I simply told him the truth: being a Protestant, it was likely I would be attacked by Catholics before I reached the hospital. I needed the knife for my own protection.

He stared into my face and after a few tense moments he handed me the flowers back, looked at the knife again, before handing it back to me as well. I breathed a sigh of relief. For a moment I had thought, "Crumlin Road here I come."

With a big smile I said thanks and walked away, at a fast trot down the street. Before turning the corner I chanced a look back and saw that the soldier was still watching me. I hoped he hadn't changed his mind.

Over the next few months my wife eventually came to accept the situation. She knew I couldn't leave the Organisation now even if I had wanted to. It never entered my mind to try and get out; I believed it was a good cause and it was only right to fight for what I believed in.

Looking back, I realised I had not really counted the cost nor did I know the price I would have to pay. I never once thought my marriage would break up, but it did. Sadly many marriages break up because a husband serves prison time.

Many people tried to talk to me about my crazy lifestyle, but I refused to listen to anyone. I never thought about the future, I just lived one day at a time. Besides, I didn't know anyone who had walked away from the UVF and lived long enough to boast about it. I continued to work at my old job but became more active in the Organisation. I even used my home to store weapons for the UVF.

All I thought about was the Protestant cause, and fighting the Republican movement!

CHAPTER SIX

BANK ROBBERY

"*T*his is a good day to rob a bank," I thought. I was aware of the sawn-off shotgun under my suit jacket, it was uncomfortable. I was hoping none of the other people standing at the bus stop would notice it. I watched the bank for several weeks. Every morning the banker did the same routine: he opened the doors, turned off the alarm, and came back out into a hall to collect the mail. I thought the hall would be the best place to jump him. I planned to run into the hallway, shove a gun into his ribs and walk him back inside the bank. Other members of my team would then help me sack up all the money in the bank. I had rehearsed this over and over with the other members of the team; everyone knew what part they were to play. I was anxious for the guy to arrive. What was keeping him?

That morning as I stood waiting for the banker to arrive I was shocked when I heard someone call out, "Packie are you not going to work today?" It was my boss. I couldn't believe it! He had pulled up in his car to offer me a ride to work and was talking to me through the car window. It was difficult for me to bend over to answer him because of the gun under my coat.

"I have to go somewhere but I will be in this afternoon," I whispered. I didn't want to talk to him so I said, "You're holding up traffic. I'll see you later." I was glad when he said, "OK, see you this afternoon." I breathed a sigh of relief and looked over at my mates standing across the street. They were dressed as painters, holding buckets and cans of paint—only it wasn't paint inside the buckets, it was guns!

They stared at me, waiting for me to start the operation. I looked back at the bank and thought I had missed my opportunity. The lights were on; while I had been talking to my boss the banker had arrived! A few moments later he went out into the hall. As he bent over to the pick up the mail I ran up the steps, kicked him down to the floor and stuck the gun into his face.

"Don't even breathe," I said. I grabbed him by the hair and shoved him into the foyer of the bank. We could not be seen from the outside because the windows were laminated with plastic half-way up. I signalled for my team members to come and join me just as we had planned. The banker then followed my instructions to lock the doors again.

We tried to open the night safe. Unfortunately the keys to the safe were kept by another employee who had yet to arrive. We decided to wait for him. One by one, other employees of the bank began to arrive. The manager and I let them in the front door and put them into a separate room out at the back where one of our gang held them at gun-point.

A few minutes later something happened I wasn't expecting, I heard a noise at the window and when I looked up I saw the top of a ladder. I could not believe what I was seeing: someone was actually beginning to climb up it!

This was not part of our plan; it was a real window cleaner! I grabbed the manager and told him to go outside and call the window cleaner to come into the bank. I warned the banker that if he tried anything else I would shoot him first. I was relieved when the window cleaner came in. I told him what was going on and put him in the next room with the other hostages.

By now we had been in the bank almost an hour. I knew our getaway driver would be beside himself. We finally got both safes open and filled briefcases with money. I let most of the team out through the front door again. The two of us who remained would leave by the back door with the money. As we walked to our car, an army patrol suddenly turned the corner and came directly towards us. I tried to act like a businessman and spoke to the army officer, "Not a bad day is it?" Obviously they were not suspicious of us and we walked by them to our waiting car.

Sometimes truth is stranger than fiction. What happened next is hard to believe. Two days after the bank robbery I was on the job as a welder for my company that manufactured gates, security rails, and fire-escape stairs. My boss called me and said, "Get into the car. We're going to measure a job. We have to make some security grills for a bank."

I recognised the route we were taking as the same route to the bank that I had robbed two days before.

Sure enough we stopped outside the bank and I balked. "I can't go in there! No way can I go in there!"

My boss looked at me and his expression changed. "Don't tell me you robbed this bank the other day!"

I said, "OK, I won't tell you then, but I can't go in there!"

We drove back to work and my boss went back to the bank with someone else. I knew my boss was now aware of my involvement with the Organisation but he was afraid to say anything to me about it. He knew it could cost him his life.

A few months later I robbed a post office. My friend and I walked in with guns and ordered everyone to lie on the floor. While my friend held a gun on them, I jumped over the counter and emptied the money from the tills. Within two minutes we were out of the post office and escaped in a stolen car. I casually went to get a haircut and on to work. Robberies were becoming a regular part of my life now.

A similar coincidence occurred the afternoon of the post office robbery. I went to the home of my boss so I had an alibi in case I needed one. His friend, a post office worker, came through the front door shouting about getting robbed that morning. He said he was frightened because he had £300 in his hand when the robbers entered the post office. When he was told to lie on the floor, he lay on top of the money. He smiled at me and said, "I'd love to see that gunman's face if he knew he missed that money."

I tried to smile back at him and thought to myself, "Mister if you only knew the truth, you wouldn't be laughing now!" Little did he know it was that gunman he was telling his story to!

In the back of my mind I always thought I would eventually be caught by the police and returned to prison. However I did not let my mind dwell on that possibility and never talked to my wife about what lay ahead: I didn't care—I didn't want to stop. I believed in what I was doing. It was for the Protestant cause!

My worst fears came true. One night the security forces raided our house moments after I arrived home. I ran out the back door and vaulted into a hedgerow to hide. One of the policemen spotted me and hand-cuffed me on the ground. I was defiant and shouted over my shoulder to my wife, "Don't worry! I'll be back soon." I had a flashback. That's what I had said to her the last time I was arrested. She remembered too.

One of the policemen shook his head and said, "Son, it's going to be a long, long time before you're back."

I didn't answer him but had a strange feeling that he was telling the truth. He was! This time it would be five years before I would see my old neighbour-hood again.

CHAPTER SEVEN

BACK IN PRISON!

My second time in prison was a nightmare, especially those first few months. You can't stop thinking about outside. Constantly your thoughts are, *What would I be doing now if I were out?* or —especially at the weekend—*Where would I be tonight if I were out?* These are the thoughts of most single men for the first six months after being locked up. Then "inside" becomes your normal lifestyle and you kind of forget about what you did when you were free. But for the married man it's worse: you think: *Will my marriage survive?* You just don't know. My thoughts changed too, *I wonder where she is tonight; will she be out to the bar? Who's she with?* Such thoughts almost drive you crazy! I saw many married men crack up; they were seen as tough guys outside, but they couldn't cope with the pressures of being inside.

Most married men who go into gaol have this fear. Although they may not acknowledge it, I believe it lingers in the back of their minds. Most of my weekends on the outside were spent drinking with the boys. I never went shopping with my wife Maxine, and only rarely did I take her out for a drink. I would use the excuse "If I had more money I'd take you out more," but in reality I preferred to be out with my friends rather than with her. A lot of times I would stay away all weekend and come home on Sunday evening. But then, I didn't see it as being wrong really. I knew it wasn't good either, but I always made sure my wife got her share of my wages. So to me that made it all right.

I remember having a conversation one day with my wife while I was in remand: "At least we had a good relationship outside." I suggested and was shocked by her answer. "It was good for you, not for me. You think because you sent money home to feed us that made a good relationship. We had no relationship, you just did your own thing." I was hearing the hard truth now. "Why didn't you tell me this outside?" I asked. She shook her head and answered, "David, I tried to, but you never took the time to listen to me."

We were allowed three half-hour visits per week while I waited for sentencing. The visits were the highlight of my week. I missed most the privacy I had enjoyed with my wife. Privacy is a foreign word in prison. It was hard to talk with my wife about any serious subject because another prisoner and his visitor were just a metre away listening to everything said. There were times I watched my wife leave in tears, because of the lack of privacy and the tension we felt knowing others heard everything we said. Every prisoner knew the feeling. Most of the time the conversation is only small talk; you can't say what is really on your mind and you can't express how you really feel. This applies to the wives as well as the husbands. Many times I've seen a prisoner return to his cell with his head hung low and not speak to anyone. The usual comment, if any, would be, "He's had a bad visit."

It seemed impossible for any marriage to survive with one partner in prison for a long time. I can count on my hands the small number of marriages that did last. After sentencing, visits were limited to just 30 minutes per week. That's only 26 hours per year to talk to your wife, the equivalent of slightly more than one day. I knew the chances of my marriage surviving were slim. I had not been able to maintain a good relationship on the outside; how could I survive an eleven year stretch on 30 minutes each week? This is when you know you're doing Time.

That's why visitation was always a point of contention between prisoners and the authorities. On another occasion a full-scale riot broke out because visits were cancelled after the IRA murdered a prison governor as he had just left the prison. I had actually spoken to him just before lunch; he had passed through the prison laundry and saw me with a note in my hand—he thought it must be a smuggled note from a prisoner in another part of the gaol so he asked to see it. In fact all it was a note of my laundry wash, to inform me which item of clothing belonged to whom. It was hard for me to believe that this poor man was murdered just a few hours later.

Because of this we were kept locked up in our cells (this is the usual procedure for all prisons in Northern Ireland). The following day was Saturday and lot of guys were expecting a visit, but they were cancelled too. Many of the prisoners' families and friends had travelled quite a distance only to find the visits cancelled. That made a lot of men very unhappy. When we eventually got out of our cells to go down to the canteen for our supper a lot of guys were shouting that we should protest, so we decided not to lock up again until we got to speak to the wing governor to voice our complaint. After almost an hour of shouting, the governor arrived. He came into the dining hall and told us to lock up or else. He refused to even give us a hearing but insisted we go back to our cells. I was really angry at this point and as he turned to walk out I lifted my chair and threw it at his back. This was all some of the guys needed to react; within seconds the place was being smashed up. I jumped up onto the table and started to smash the lights. Tables were over turned and legs were broken off as weapons. At this point I just didn't care what the consequences were. I just vented my anger and frustration. As always I expressed myself the way I knew best, which was with violence.

We built barricades with the broken tables and chairs in front of the iron gates to prevent the riot squad from entering the area. Quietness settled down over the entire prison. We knew it was the calm before the storm. Surely the screws were planning to attack us, most likely through the large steel door at the top of the dining hall. A screeching sound told us that the bar that held the door was being pulled back. The door swung open. Someone shouted, "Get ready, they're coming in the top door!"

I turned and faced the doorway and looked through gaps in the barricade. I held a steel table leg in one hand and three darts in the other. I was shocked when I realised the faces I saw were not prison officers. It was the army! A soldier put a rubber-bullet gun through the bars, took aim, and fired at me. The bullet hit me in the shoulder and spun me around. We all tried to find cover behind chairs or tables. I turned and threw the three darts toward the crowd of soldiers and officers who were charging us. Suddenly I was knocked to the floor by a strong jet of cold water. I could hardly breathe. I thought I would drown if the water didn't stop. I gasped for air and felt the heel of a boot on my throat. I choked as I looked past the boot to see a soldier enjoying his conquest of me. He raised the visor on his helmet and gave me an evil smile. He took a rubber bullet out of his belt, loaded his gun, and placed the muzzle within two inches of my face. I heard the click as he cocked the gun.

"Please, mister, don't!" I begged. He smiled again and moved the gun down pointing it between my legs. I pleaded with him not to shoot me. He moved the gun to my thigh and pulled the trigger. The pain was unbearable. My leg felt like it was on fire, as if someone had stuck a hot poker into me. I thought for sure it was broken. The force of the shot spun me around on the floor. As I cried out in pain an officer came across the room and kicked me and told me to stand against the wall. Some of my friends helped me to my feet and prevented me from falling.

I stood on one leg with my nose pressed against the wall. If we looked around, a soldier used a baton across the back of our heads or crushed our fingers on the wall. One by one we were led into the "bunk", a cell used by prison staff as an office. There we met the prison doctor, famous for standing by the wall with his hands behind him. I never knew anyone who had ever been actually examined by him.

The doctor asked me, "What's wrong with you?"

I knew from my past experience with the doctor what his standard answer would be: "You need a three-day lockup." So I knew not to expect any help from the doctor. My thigh was swollen to twice its normal size—it was obvious what my problem was.

"Let's see this leg; pull your trousers down," the doctor impatiently requested. My thigh was black and blue and there was a perfect circle where the bullet hit me. He asked, "How did you do this?" I told him about the soldier but he chose not to believe me.

His conclusion was that the wound was self-inflicted and that I needed to be locked up for a few days.

I was expecting this kind of response from him, so I just said, "Thanks, doc, it's nice to know someone cares!" I held onto the wall and walked out of the cell.

A screw said, "Now is when the fun starts, Hamilton! You have to run the gauntlet." I looked down the wing and saw what he meant.

Prison officers were lined up double all the way to the bottom of the stairs. They would issue their own punishment to us! I just smiled at him. I can honestly say I wasn't the least bit afraid—violence and pain were a big part of my life; you just accept it. Outside, whenever the Police would have you in a cell, most times they would give you a beating. Whenever they beat me, I grew more determined not to break. So most times the beatings actually caused me to hate authority even more.

I made no attempt to run; I could barely walk; I started to pass through the middle of them; some of them were screaming in delight as they began to beat me with their batons. I tried to protect my face as best I could. I felt blood running down my neck after a strong blow to the head. Eventually I reached the bottom of the stairs; my beating stopped at the same time I heard someone behind me scream as the screws began to batter him. I struggled to the top of the landing and limped to my cell.

I wiped the blood off with my towel and changed into dry clothes. I collapsed on my bed and looked across at my cell-mate. He had a wet face cloth over his face.

"How many bumps have you?" he asked, with a laugh. He stopped laughing when he saw the mess my leg was in. He couldn't believe it. Today, seventeen years later, I still carry the indent in my thigh where that soldier shot me with that rubber bullet.

It took quite a while for things to settle down. Some prisoners collected names of the screws who did most of the beatings and these were sent out to paramilitaries to be dealt with. One of the worst officers involved was a Welshman; he *enjoyed* beating you with a truncheon. He would scream in delight as he battered you. If anyone was a sadist he fitted the description. I cannot say it was a surprise to me to learn he was shot a few weeks later. Fortunately for him, he survived it.

I was glad when my trial date was finally set. I spent a lot of time talking to my barrister about the trial. He told me I would probably be sentenced to at least five years more than the others who had been involved with me in the bank and post office robberies. He thought the others might get up to ten years and that I would get hit even harder.

When I walked into the courtroom I wasn't terribly pleased to find out the judge was the same judge who sentenced me a few years before. That was all I needed! My brain was overwhelmed by the memory of the judge telling me he never wanted to see me again ...

The judge first sentenced my friend. He got 12 years! My mind was racing, *if he got 12 years (It was later reduced to 11 years), how many would I get?* I was calculating in my head—if my barrister was right, I would be serving a 16-18 year stretch!!

When the judge called out my name, I stood up, expecting the worst. It seemed like an eternity as all my charges were read out. I had already pleaded guilty; now I would know the sentence. I got five years for this, then eight years for that; ten years for something else, I wasn't so much interested in the charges, it was the sentences I was listening to. The longest sentence, that would be the one that I would have to serve. What about my five-year licence? As I feared, the judge made reference to it before he announced his final decision. Some of our relatives were crying in the public gallery by this stage.

"Hamilton," the judge started slowly, "It's obvious you all relied a lot on teamwork to accomplish these crimes. Therefore I feel it would be wrong of me to sentence you to more than the others. I sentence you to 12 years also!"

Back in the cells beneath the courts the screw removed my handcuffs. My mate banged the wall with his fist, "That judge was bad news." Our barrister came to the cell with a sheepish look on his face: he couldn't explain the long sentences. He said the judge showed no leniency at all, except to me. He turned to me and said "You got off light—you should be happy" I answered "You don't see me laughing, do you?" He looked me straight in the eyes and said, "You should be: someone must have been praying for you."

I grumbled, "I don't think so."

Years later I would find out that someone had been praying for me, a precious old woman whose prayers would change my life.

CHAPTER EIGHT

PACKIE THE PRISONER

The moment we were sentenced we were told we would no longer be treated as political prisoners. Now we were seen as real criminals and had to wear prison uniforms (Political status had been cancelled by this time). I was moved to the Maze prison, commonly known as the H-Blocks. All newly sentenced prisoners were housed in block H-7. I did not know what to expect; it had the reputation of being very strict.

The guards let us know who was in charge of the place. The block was kept immaculately clean; the tile floor was constantly washed, polished and buffed. The toilets were kept spotless, even the toilet seats were polished. The black plastic bins were also given the same treatment so that they were gleaming too. This was the discipline block, specifically set up to teach prisoners strict discipline. We were constantly reminded that we were now sentenced prisoners, criminals. No longer political prisoners, no more special privileges, you did whatever the screws told you to do.

The block was built in the shape of the letter "H", with four wings. The centre bar was for the administration office. I didn't like living in "The Blocks" at all. The exercise yard was depressing; it was a square yard enclosed on every side by corrugated fencing four metres high. You could see nothing, only four tin walls. A highlight for us was to see an aeroplane flying high across the sky; it helped to break the monotony. Exercise was like walking around the inside of a huge biscuit tin.

After a month in the discipline block I was moved to H-6 where life was a little easier. I got allocated a job in the prison laundry and I was happy about this. It was a good number because it had plenty of perks.

It meant I was able to wear the best of prison garb including a denim waistcoat over my blue and white pinstripe shirt and grey denim trousers. As a laundry worker I had a little more freedom than the normal prisoner as I had to pick up and deliver laundry. I enjoyed my visits to the prison kitchen because I usually came back with more than dirty clothes.

One day I filled the laundry bag with all kinds of goodies. As I walked toward the laundry the PO (principal officer) stopped me.

"Let me see inside your bag," he ordered.

I didn't know what to do. I knew I was in big trouble and would probably be sent to "the boards", the slang expression for the punishment block. I fumbled with the string on the bag until food started falling out. A whole cooked chicken was followed by six eggs, two tomatoes, an onion, a half-loaf of bread and three huge chunks of corned beef!

The PO went berserk! He started shouting, "Get out of my kitchen! Don't ever come back in here! Do you hear me?"

"Yes sir!" I yelled and rushed off toward the gate. The guard opened the grill as he saw me coming, "Hamilton, you're lucky he let you off." After that experience, I always sent another prisoner to collect the kitchen laundry.

It wasn't only with the prison staff that I sometimes had problems; other times it was with the leaders of my own paramilitary group—like the time I took a notion to carve an Irish harp (I really enjoy handi-crafts). I worked as an orderly at that time. One day I was sent out to clean a classroom. The blackboard on the wall was enclosed by a mahogany wood surround and I thought, "That wood would make a nice harp!" I cut all the wood off the blackboard and smuggled it into my cell. I learned the next day that both the prison authorities and the prisoners' council were upset and had begun an investigation . . . the trail led directly to my cell.

The authorities left it up to my fellow prisoners to deal with. I was told to remain locked in my cell until a court-martial trial could be set up. I was charged with destroying prisoners' property, a severe offence. That afternoon I was taken to the classroom and met by four prisoners sitting at a table. The four were in charge of each of the wings of our block. I was worried because one of these men was considered to be the top man of all the loyalists in the Maze. He had murdered several people both inside and outside of prison. It was rumoured that he poisoned his cell-mate the year before. I didn't think I would be killed for stealing the wood from around the blackboard, but I was still nervous as to what my punishment might be.

I sat down and one of the men said, "As you can see Packie, there's no blackboard in here. We were wondering if you know where it could be?"

I told them the truth. They asked me to wait outside while they decided my punishment. When they called me back inside, the main man, said, "We've decided to give you the benefit of the doubt. You're new here and we're letting you off light. Your punishment is to be locked up for a week, no recreation, no yard time." I was thankful that my first brush with prison justice ended OK.

Being locked up was no problem. I spent the time in my cell working on my harp. No one had mentioned the wood, so I kept it!

I made many friends in the H-Blocks. About the time I began feeling at home I was transferred to Belfast Prison, the "Crum." I was placed in "D" wing, the one reserved for prisoners serving long sentences. It was not a happy place! Some of the most hardened criminals were in "D" wing, including sex offenders who would have been beaten or killed in the Blocks.

I felt all eyes on me at supper that night. I was the new kid on the block. I felt better when a guy shouted, "Packie, bring your grub over here and sit down." It was a prisoner named Edge, one of the top men in the prison. We had served a term together a few years before. It was important to be recognised. It gave me status. I was pleased to see some of my friends I had not seen in years, especially some of my homeboys from my own neighbourhood.

I had a slight problem my very first night in the "Crum." I was put into a cell with a crazy guy who woke me up in the middle of the night standing over me with his pants down. I was mad! I punched him until my knuckles were sore. I kicked him until my toes hurt. He screamed like a pig. When a Screw opened the door the next morning he saw the guy's face. I said, "He fell during the night and busted his face. He wants to move to another cell. I don't want him sleeping here tonight." That afternoon he was moved.

It was easier for my wife and family to visit me in Belfast Prison since the prison was only 15 minutes from my home. I landed a job in the laundry again. I had learned the prison work ethic: do as little as you can, as often as you can. The prison laundry was old. The machines dated from the beginning of the century (which century was debatable).

We delivered laundry around the prison in huge blue baskets. It was a great way to smuggle contraband! Prisoners who wanted a special touch for their clothing paid us off in food, pornographic literature, or tobacco, the most used method of payment in prison.

The handicrafts were better in Belfast prison than the Maze: there was much more room. We had a good size workshop purely for this purpose, whereas down below we had to do crafts in a regular cell, which meant only two or three could work in it, and much of the work had to be done in your own cell. This wasn't good especially if you were sanding or sawing wood and your cell got full of sawdust. Whoever designed the H-Blocks had one thing in mind: make cells for men to stay in. He wasn't told these men would be let out to have recreation, so he didn't plan anywhere for men to work at their hobbies. I began to do leatherwork up there; it was something I got a lot of pleasure in. I paid another inmate to teach me the basics and began by making small items, such as lighter cases with guys' initials on them or made a belt to learn the stamping techniques. Then I expanded to larger items like purses with beautiful carved designs. These became really popular—some of the leather work that came out of the prisons in Northern Ireland are real works of art, the carving techniques acknowledged by leatherworkers around the world!

Over the years I've made everything from Bible covers to gun holsters. It was common for officers to ask someone to make handbags or other things for their wives. There were only a few master workers who each had their own secrets but over the years they taught me. It was a great way to pass the time away.

CHAPTER NINE

RECEIVING LIFE!

"*A*ny volunteers to read a prayer?" the prison chaplain, Rev. Robert Russell asked during the Thursday afternoon chapel service (we went to church just to have something to do). No one volunteered to pray. Someone shouted, "The last time I volunteered for anything I got ten years in prison!" Everyone laughed. The chaplain looked straight at me and asked, "How about you Packie?" I would try anything once so I told him OK. He handed me a small piece of paper with a prayer poem written on it. When I stood up to read it one of my mates grabbed the back of my leg to make me scream. Somehow I managed not to!

When I finished reading the prayer I felt good inside. I couldn't explain it. I wrote to my mother that night and told her how good it was to say a prayer in church. Only God could have known that in less than a year I would be doing much more than praying in church.

I heard that my friend Billy had become a Christian. He was a bit crazy anyway, only now he was completely crazy. No one I knew in gaol was interested in God. We went to church to hear "all the scale" (new news) not because any one had time for God. I couldn't see big Billy staying a Christian for long. I just laughed.

I remember that New Year's eve. I was sharing a cell with a crazy guy with the nickname Crazy Horse. That night a few minutes before midnight we took our steel feet off our beds to bang the steel door with—this was our way of seeing the new year in. It is a time of festivity, so even in gaol we celebrate it. At the stroke of midnight as car horns are sounded all across the city and the ships in the harbour are blowing their huge horns, all the prisoners usually shout out the side of the doors and make as much noise as possible.

I can remember standing at the door banging it as hard as I could. I thought to myself, *This new year will be no different from last year or the year before.* Things never change in any big way in the prison, even the food is the same each week. Yet before the first month of the new year would be over, my life would be changed completely.

It was the 28th January 1980. As always, I got myself a cup of hot water to bring into my cell, to make a cup of tea. We were banging up for the night.

When I pulled my cell door shut, I saw a small piece of paper lying on my bed. I asked my cell-mate what it was. He told me it was a Christian tract. I just laughed, picked it up, looked at the front page, and read it out loud, "Jesus Christ is coming back soon," I turned and said to my cell-mate, " To a cinema near you!" We both laughed.

Like most guys in jail, I wasn't interested in anything to do with religion. So I screwed the tract up into a ball, and threw it out the window. I sat down on my bed to drink my tea and never gave the tract any more thought.

While I was sitting there something strange happened. This thought came into my mind, *It's time for you to change, to become a Christian.* I was startled by this; it was so strange. Never in my life had I ever thought to be a Christian. I took another gulp of tea. A few moments later again I had the same thought, *Become a Christian.* This time I laughed out loud and my cell-mate asked, "What are you laughing about?"

"Nothing." I answered, He wouldn't believe me if I told him, so I said nothing. Even if I wanted to be a real Christian I thought for sure God would not be interested in someone like me. I thought I was too far gone to ever change. I knew I was bad, and I'd been involved in some bad things. The Organisation I belonged to had killed many people.

Some of my best friends were murderers. It wasn't because they were any worse than me, it was just the way things happened to turn out. I had not taken anyone's life, but it wasn't for the want of trying. I knew it was a miracle that I was not serving a life sentence too. I could recall times when I left my house with murder on my mind. Now I can say I am truly thankful to God it never took place.

But I knew I was a violent man at times and also a robber and a thief. Surely God had no time for people like me!

I shook myself back to reality and put my cup upon the bookshelf, beside a Bible. (There is a Bible in every cell, thanks to a Christian organisation called Gideons International, who distribute Bibles into schools, hotels and prisons in most of the countries of the world).

In fact, all the guys in gaol like the Bible; if you run out of cigarette papers it's the next best thing—you just rip a page out of it! I guess I'd smoked Matthew, Mark, Luke and John over the years!

I looked at the Bible as if seeing it for the first time, I lifted it down and began to flick the pages, reading a few lines here and there; it didn't make any sense at all so I put it back on the shelf. A few minutes later, I pulled it back down again, opened it and tried to read for the second time. It still didn't make much sense, so I put it back again. I really felt uncomfortable, as if something was bothering me. I was starting to feel agitated for no reason.

I sat back on my bed looking at this Bible, then I thought to myself, *Didn't I hear the Minister say you should always pray before reading the Bible?* So I lifted the Bible down, sat back on the bed with the Bible sitting on my knees and I actually prayed a silent prayer asking God to help me read the Bible. That was all I prayed. I opened it for the third time and began to read and after a few lines it still didn't seem to make any sense.

"What are you doing with that Bible?" Crazy Horse asked. I didn't know what to answer. Sheepishly, I said, "I am thinking about being a Christian."

Of course he began to laugh, "You a Christian?! No way." he lay back on his bed laughing, "You need a good night's sleep you will be normal again tomorrow."

I was in the middle of a snooker competition and I had actually reached the finals, it was between a guy called Jojo and me to see who would win the prize of tobacco. Before lock-up it was the only thing on my mind, now it didn't seem to be of any importance if I won or not. I thought, *My mate is right, this is crazy, tomorrow I will have forgotten all about this*. So I rolled a cigarette and lay back on the bed.

Anyway God would have no time for the likes of me he's only interested in good people the sort who go to church and listen to "Batman". (As a child, when I first went to church and saw the minister all dressed up in black, even with a robe! I thought it was batman; two years later I found out it wasn't—man, was I disappointed).

While lying on my bed I started to think about my life; the way I lived outside. Now it seemed it was crazy. Maybe there is a better way to live, but where do you find it? As a Christian? I doubted that; it had no appeal to me at all. Prison was bad, but church was worse! No life in being a Christian: I reasoned that it must be terribly boring to be a Christian, no more smoking, drinking, sleeping around or partying.

My next thought was those things never truly satisfy anyway. Then I began to have these strange thoughts about times in my life when I could have died. I thought about the night when I was out with my fiancée having a meal and the IRA attempted to kill me; for sure that was a near miss.

I was lucky, or so I thought, maybe it was more than luck. What about the time my bomb exploded prematurely while I was still in the building! I thought about that night, how I woke lying on the ground, broken glass all around me. Although my jacket was cut to shreds, I couldn't find so much as a scratch on my body. How did I survive that? *It must have been God!*

What about the time I was shot while up the Shankill? Three bullets in me! Not many live to tell such tales, so why was I still alive? The thought rushed through my brain, *It WAS God who kept me alive, all those times.* There was really no other explanation, but why? If God wasn't interested in people like me, then surely he would have let me die. So what was the reason for sparing my life? What could it be? Could God change my life after all?

I was feeling confused now, and these thoughts continued until I finally fell asleep.The next morning when I awoke, my first thought was *Become a Christian.* The thoughts were still there! I knew I had to make some kind of a decision soon because this Christian thing was beginning to bother me now. I still felt it was time for me to change but I didn't know exactly how to do that. But I was soon to discover that God always puts people in our pathway to help us find His will for our lives. The right person for me was close by! I worked in the prison laundry with a man nicknamed the "Wee Man". Trev (Trevor was his proper name) had been a Christian for eight years and was famous for sticking gospel tracts inside trouser and shirt pockets in the laundry. I admired him because he had the guts to distribute the tracts, but I still thought he was crazy. Many times I had seen him put gospel tracts inside the clothes. This would make men mad. Many times they would threaten him to try to make him stop, but the "Wee Man" just kept on. He always carried gospel tracts in his pockets. Once I saw a guard take his hat off and set it down on the table to wipe his brow with a handkerchief—it was always hot and steamy in the laundry. The "Wee Man" moved over close to the table. Next thing he stuck something inside the brim of the screw's hat and walked away. A minute later when the guard placed his hat back on his head he immediately took it off again to see what was inside. From out of the brim he pulled out a gospel tract! I thought it was so funny!

As I was going down to go to work that morning someone was blocking the stairs. It was the "Wee Man". He turned and spoke to me. The next words out of my mouth surprised even me, "Wee Man, I'm thinking about becoming a Christian, but I don't know what to do". I thought he would laugh at me because I had mocked him so many times for being a Christian. Instead he walked up to me and put his arms around me and hugged me. I was embarrassed and glad none of the other prisoners were around. That kind of action is easily misinterpreted in prison. The "Wee Man" gave me several tracts, enough reading material for a month!

During a break in the laundry, I asked the "Wee Man" questions about being a Christian. Someone shouted, "Look at Packie talking to the Sky Pilot." ("Sky Pilot" was one of our mocking names for Christians). I was embarrassed and asked the "Wee Man" to meet me in the toilet to talk. The "Wee Man" prayed with me and asked God to show me how to get saved; before he left, he gave me more tracts. I went back to my cell and during lunch made up my mind that it was time to turn my life over to Christ. I read one of the Wee Man's tracts that had a simple prayer,

> Come into my heart Lord Jesus,
> Come into my heart today,
> Come into my heart Lord Jesus,
> Come into my heart to stay.

I prayed the prayer six times just to make sure God knew I was serious! "That's it!" I thought. "I'm now a Christian." My cell-mate woke up and asked me what I was smiling about. I said, "I've just become a Christian." He snarled at me and used a few curse words to tell me how he felt about my decision. When the cell door opened for us to return to work he started yelling, "Packie's a Christian now! He's joined the God Squad." Another prisoner shouted, "Hallelujah!" The first person I saw was Jojo whom I was supposed to play in a snooker game that night. I told him, "Jojo, I can't play snooker tonight because it's for tobacco, it's gambling and Christians don't gamble." He laughed and walked on without answering. Someone else yelled out, "Tonight Packie will perform his first miracle, he's going to walk on the bath water!" A lot of guys were laughing now. So was I!

That afternoon, on the way over to work, I spotted the Chaplain, Rev. Bill Vance. I shouted over to him " I am a Christian now." He stopped and walked back to me, "When did this happen?" he asked. He then told me to follow him back to the wing. In the office he asked me to tell him what happened, so I told him as best I could. He just sat and smiled; when I'd finished he got up, opened a cupboard and gave me my first Bible, a little red New Testament. He prayed for me before I went back to the laundry. I felt ten feet tall. It was the first time I heard anyone personally praying for me.

What I didn't know then was that God had someone else praying for David Hamilton's salvation. He had placed me on the heart of an 83-year-old lady named Annie Beggs, my uncle's mother-in-law. I never knew Mrs. Beggs personally before my conversion—as a boy occasionally I would hear my mum mention her in conversation—but she knew me OK! On the day I was sentenced to prison she spoke to my mother who was sitting crying about her hopeless son. Mum said I was a hopeless case, that all I lived for was the UVF, and that I would never change.

Mrs. Beggs shook her head and told mum, "God can change your son." Mum disagreed and shook her head in despair. Mrs. Beggs continued, "If God could change the heart of John Newton (who after his conversion composed the hymn *Amazing Grace),* he can change the heart of your son. I will put him on my prayer list and pray for him every day, I promise you," she said.

At that time she was in her eighties. An amazing woman for her age, she had all her faculties about her, spending most of her nights in prayer.

When she said she was praying about something she meant it. She was known by many as a woman of prayer. A well-known professor in a Belfast hospital would come to seek her advice on many things, because once he himself had to go into hospital for heart surgery. He was unsure because the medical people had told him it had only a 50% chance of working. It could actually go either way. Annie told him she would pray about it first and then let him know what she thought he should do.

She later told him she had prayed and God had given her assurance it would be successful and she felt he should go ahead with the operation, which he did. It was a great success and amazed the surgeon and staff involved in the operation, as they watched the speed of his recovery. The professor said it was because Annie Beggs had been praying for him.

Two years later God miraculously answered the prayers of Annie Beggs, this time on my behalf. When I got converted, it was the talk of the whole wing. I knew that I would be the butt of all the jokes when I showed up in the dining hall that evening. Sure enough Jojo stood up on a chair and announced, "Since Packie is a Christian now he can pray for our food!" Everyone laughed, except me. I was a nice shade of purple. Above the laughter he said, "Everyone bow your heads, all eyes closed. Packie pray!" I set my tray down on the table in front of me, bowed my head and said a short prayer. When I opened my eyes I discovered my sausages were gone from off my tray. It didn't stop me praying though, I continued to pray for all my meals after that, but I always made sure I kept one eye open.

That night I wrote to my parents to tell them about my conversion. I later found out that my mother had cried as she read my letter out, and my Father was almost crying too. He said, "Poor son, he's went mad in prison." My mother was so moved that she made a decision for Christ two days later. She could hardly wait to visit Granny Beggs (as my mum called her) to tell her the good news. Before mum could tell Granny anything, Granny said, "I know why you're here! David has become a Christian." She told mum that God had lifted the burden for my salvation from her heart the night I got saved. "Now," she added "God has told me to pray for his future ministry."

I went to my first prison prayer meeting a few days after I got saved. I was embarrassed because there were several prisoners there whom I had ridiculed in a terrible way for their stand as Christians, just three nights before. I knew they did not take me serious—they found it hard to accept that I was truly converted.

There were several sex-offenders present in the meeting. I couldn't accept them either as being Christians and they knew it. About the only person glad to see me was the Chaplain, the Rev. David Jardine who announced, "It's nice to see you, David. Take a seat. We're reading from Galatians." I often tried to be witty so I asked, "Is that some place in Belfast?" I was the only person laughing. One of the men turned to his friend and said, "I knew he wasn't saved."

I felt stupid for not being more serious. I made another blunder about 15 minutes later. I was so relaxed in the Bible study that I took a cigarette tin out of my pocket and began to roll a smoke. All eyes were on me. I thought, "This is not right. A Christian shares things with others and I haven't even offered anyone else a cigarette." So I stood up and offered my tin around. I was surprised when no one accepted.

"David you can't smoke in here. This is a Bible study," the chaplain said kindly. "Oh," I replied and put the blow (cigarette) behind my ear for later. I heard your man make another comment, "Told you he wasn't saved."

I just smiled. I knew I had a lot to learn now as a Christian.

CHAPTER TEN

A PRISON CHRISTIAN

Life in prison is tough at the best of times, but as a Christian it was even tougher. I began to make some new Christian friends while a few fellow prisoners despised me for no longer being a Loyalist. I had made a decision immediately to stop being a member of the UVF. Regardless of the consequences, I felt it was the only thing to do. The truth was I had to leave now or I could not call myself a Christian.

I cancelled my financial support from them on the outside. I stopped having visits from anyone who was involved with the organisation outside.

I told them I was finished with it all: no more taking orders; I would talk to everybody from now on. I soon found out, although God had changed me, he hadn't changed everyone else. There was a Catholic guy I had had a fight with, one time, over in the laundry, and since then we stayed out of each other's way. But the same day I made my commitment to Christ, I went to him and told him. His answer was "Why are you telling me this?" I told him from now on I will be speaking to everyone. I don't care who they are, or what their crime was. One man, Big D, challenged me to stop smoking, He said it would prove to others that I was serious about serving God. I accepted the challenge. Thank God, I've never had a cigarette since. I know it was a miracle for me to stop smoking, since I had tried several times before but never succeeded. I knew this time it wasn't my own strength I was depending on. I had no craving, unlike the previous times—I didn't even feel tempted for a cigarette.

I was in a guy's cell three days later, when he offered me a cigarette, I refused it and said, "As a Christian now, I don't smoke." He laughed at me and said, "Packie, don't go overboard; as a Christian you can still smoke, you know." My reply was "The Apostle Peter went overboard and he walked on water! So I want to go all the way too." He had a good laugh over this.

Big D was a genuine Christian. We became good friends and later on cell-mates. He taught me a lot about studying the Bible and applying the principles I learned to my everyday life, even locked up in a prison. Big D was completely opposite from me. I never cared about how my cell looked but Big D kept the cell immaculate. He even folded his socks before putting them in the cupboard. His side of the bookshelf was clean, mine was full of cobwebs.

I was in the exercise yard a few days later when one of my friends came over to me and announced, "Packie, I think you're a genuine Christian. Keep it up, I'm betting a half-ounce on you!" I found out that many prisoners were betting on how long I would last as a Christian.

It scared me a little, and I confided in my friend Jamie that I didn't think I would make it as a Christian. Although I wanted to, I just couldn't see myself lasting as one; I was not strong enough. I was shocked by his answer, "You're right Packie, you don't have the strength. But God does!" He turned to John 1:12 in his Bible which reads, "To as many as believe in Him, God gives them the power to become a son of God." That's what I needed to hear.

The Devil doesn't like to let anyone go that easily, as I soon found out. One of the screws came into my cell and asked me if I was still a Christian. When I replied "Yeah" with a smile, he punched me in the face. I was determined not to react, "Are you still a Christian?" He asked and punched me again, laughed in my face, turned and walked out the door. That officer hated me from that day on. He never accepted that my conversion was real. Even when I was eventually released from prison he told me on my way out that he would keep my cell ready because he knew I would be back! I told him I hoped he was right because I wanted to come back but this time to preach the Gospel to the men who remained locked up.

The Devil didn't stop there either. He had another go at me a week later. This time from a screw that lived in the same area as I did outside. He thought because I was a Christian now, the UVF would have nothing to do with me, or perhaps they would put me on a hit list because I no longer was a member. Whatever the reason, he decided he would give me a hard time. As I came back from work that monday lunch time, he called me over and told me to strip off. He said he wanted to search me in case I had a weapon or drugs—I knew this wasn't really the case. As I removed my outer clothing he told me to strip naked. He then made me stand there for about fifteen minutes while the other guys went past to their cells. That afternoon coming back onto the landing he called me and did the same thing again. Inside me I felt I wanted to hit him and that would put a stop to all this, but then I thought if I do that everyone will say Packie is no longer a Christian. I will be doing just what he wants me to do. I decided I would just take it and ask God to help me. Of course my mates who were watching all of this said, "Packie you're crazy, why not send his name outside and the boys will kill him for you?" I said no, "I believe God will deal with him about this." He continued to search me each day for the rest of that week and I was waiting for it to start again when I went to work the following monday morning. I was surprised when I came back onto the landing that dinner hour and he greeted me as a long lost friend. He was so nice to me, I couldn't figure out why. I knew God had answered my prayers, but what I didn't know then was that it was "with a little help from my friends". Unknown to me, one of my UVF mates decided to send this man's name out and asked someone to have a talk with him but not to kill him or I would know. It happened that weekend; this screw was out drinking with another screw in one of the local bars in our area when a few men walked into the toilet behind him and stuck a gun barrel up his nostril and asked him if he knew a friend of theirs called Packie Hamilton. They told him someone had said he was giving me a hard time—of course, he denied it. They told him if it didn't stop he would be a dead man because they knew where he lived and could get him any time they wanted. I never had any problems with him after that, but I wasn't to find all this out till a year later. Actually it was the screw who had been with him drinking that night who told me the rest of the story.

But back then, talking at the dinner table that evening with all my old mates, I said to them all, "See how God had changed this guard's heart towards me. God still works miracles today!" One of my mates called Big J answered, "Yeah, God works in mysterious ways, that's for sure." I was surprised by this, because I knew he didn't believe in God so I wondered what he meant by it. When I asked him to explain, he just smiled as he got up to leave and repeated "God works in mysterious ways"—that was all he said. It was only later when I heard the full story, that I thought back to the conversation in the dining hall and wondered if Big J knew more about it back then than I did.

Not all the screws made it tough on me. Most of them were easy to get along with and a few became real friends. Some were Christians and helped me grow in the Lord. They slipped tracts under my door and talked to me about the Bible after they finished their rounds. I thank God for the positive influence of those officers who often came along at the right moment when I needed encouragement to continue my Christian walk.

CHAPTER ELEVEN

THE OLD MAN AND THE NEW MAN

Those early days trying to be a Christian in prison were hard for me in many ways. At times I thought *I'll never make it, I am not one of those particular kind of people who are meant to be Christian.* One guy who worked along with me was always making mock of me in front of others and putting me down as an idiot for being a Christian. I usually would just ignore him and laugh it off, but after a while it began to bother me. One particular day he was showing off how strong he was, for sure he was a big guy who worked out a lot in the gym. When he saw me he said to the others he could let me hit him a punch on the face and he wouldn't even feel it. That was the wrong thing to say in front of me, since before I became a Christian I loved to fight, enjoying the buzz I used to get from it. I knew how to punch and I knew I could knock him out with one good punch if it connected on the side of his jaw.

Sad to say, I allowed the old man in me to surface and decided I wanted to have him a fight, much to his surprise. I walked over and challenged him, "Let's go out the back just you and me and everyone can wait to see who comes back in first." Unknown to him I had gone out two minutes before and put a rolling pin at the back door so I was making sure I would win. I had made up my mind, my plan was to break his two arms. It was as if something snapped in my mind and that was all I wanted to do. I hadn't had even one row since my conversion—I had been a Christian now for around three months. But now it was the "old man." I shouted at this guy who was doing all this boasting and called him every name I could think of to try to get him mad. He got afraid, having never seen me like this before, and he began to apologise and say he didn't want to fight. Eventually I walked away. It wasn't long after when I began to feel depressed about my earlier behaviour. So much for being a Christian! I blew it big time. I was glad when I saw that the officer who was on duty then was a Christian. He walked over and asked what was wrong. I told him all what had happened and afterwards he said "Let me pray for you." I was glad he did. I had lost my peace for a while, but now it was back again.

Christians are not sinless they just sin less. I am glad to say that was the only time that I can recall, when as a believer in prison I lost my witness. It takes years to build it up and only a minute to lose it. As I often say, "Don't give up on me, God hasn't finished with me yet!"

I have always enjoyed reading; it's a way of escape for many men in prison and there are certain classic thrillers that are read almost by everyone, books like *The Godfather, Exodus* and *Papillon*. One such book for me was *The Cross and The Switchblade* which tells the conversion story of Nicky Cruz who was a gang leader from the streets of New York. It's written by David Wilkerson who went on to start an organisation called Teen Challenge. I was greatly touched by reading it and thought I would love to be involved in a work like this, to watch God working in the lives of broken people and making them whole. This was what he was doing in my own life.

It was a real surprise to find the postal address of Teen Challenge in Northern Ireland on the back cover of this book. I was so touched by this work I decided to send them a small donation; so I saved up some of my wages for a few weeks (at that time we got paid the grand sum £2:50 a week) and I sent it off to them. They sent me a nice letter back and thanked me and said they would remember me in their prayers. I never thought much more about it.

Almost six years later—I wasn't long released from prison—I was introduced to this Pastor called Roy Kerr. As soon as I told him my name he immediately said to me "You sent Teen Challenge a donation about five years ago." He was the Director of Teen Challenge in Northern Ireland.

I was overwhelmed. We had only just met, yet when he heard my name he remembered my letter. We became good friends after that. He was the man who introduced me to the ministry of Teen Challenge, and got me personally involved in the work. I always love to be in this man's company: he has this gift to make you feel as if you are important. He is a real "Barnabas", an encourager if ever there was one. He would never let you leave without praying for you first. I would always come away as if I were walking ten foot tall.

There were some funny times too down in the kitchen, like the time I was frying the bread and started talking to another prisoner, telling him about how real God can be. I got so carried away I forgot to lift the bread out of the deep-fat fryers. There was black smoke billowing everywhere.

When the Guard walked across to me, I thought *I am in trouble now.* He looked down and saw the Bible in my hand and said, "I know, I know. 'Man shall not live by bread alone.' " He just turned and walked away.

As I began to read my Bible, I found it hard to put it down. Every day I started to spend hours in it. I learned about fasting and decided to miss my lunch. Even though I worked in the kitchen, it wasn't as bad as I thought it would be.

I believe God told me to make this part of my life on a regular basis. As I began to do this I could understand why the early Christians practised this discipline and saw things happen. So did I. I began to take it seriously, fasting for a whole day for the first time was a great experience to me; I found it helped me to read the Bible and to get more from it. So I made it part of my routine to fast one day a week. I chose Sunday; this was when we got our best dinner of the whole week—chicken or else a slice of steak. I wanted to give my best to God and this was to me the ultimate sacrifice. I maintained this for near three months, then I decided to fast for two days after reading that the Pharisees did this. So changing to Tuesday and Thursday, I kept this up for another three months. I found fasting to be powerful for my prayer life. Over the years I was able to increase this more and more until I could do prolonged fasts of two or three weeks, on those special occasions when I knew I needed to hear from God. As I did this, I saw many results of prayer.

It was eighteen months later I read in the Bible about new Christians being baptised in water. I kept coming across references to being baptised, and the thought came to me *That's what I need to do, to get baptised in water.* The thought stayed with me for weeks, and one day I was thinking about this while working in the kitchen, when the Governor came by doing his rounds. As he was passing me I spoke up, "Sir, may I speak with you a moment?"

He stopped dead, and his two escort officers looked at me in disbelief. It was against all the prison regulations to do such a thing. I did it on the spur of the moment—it certainly wasn't planned. I even surprised myself. The governor looked at me and said, "This is highly irregular, Hamilton. If you wish to speak to me you put a request in to do so." I quickly tried to apologise, "I am sorry Sir . . . " but before I got a chance to finish, he said, "What is it you want?"

I went on to tell him I was a Christian and felt it was important for me to be obedient to the command of Christ to be baptised. He surprised me by saying it was certainly right to do so (I found out he was actually an ordained Baptist minister). Then he asked next, "You are not hoping to get released to do this, are you Hamilton?" I laughed and said "I cannot see that happening Sir . . ." He came back to me and said, "Well, where do you suggest we hold this baptismal service?" I quickly replied "In the bath-house, Sir."

He looked at me for a moment and answered " Leave it with me I will think about it" and off he went.

Of course everyone was standing watching all this, and one of the officers said, "Hamilton you're lucky, if anyone else tried that, they would find themselves on the Boards, but not you! You must have someone up there on your side!" I had to laugh, "It certainly wasn't my idea, believe me!"

It must have been a month later; I hadn't heard a word back when, out of the blue, I was called down to see the Gov. He told me it was all planned; I was overjoyed.

"Are there any others besides you?" he asked.

By this time I had asked a number of guys if they wanted to be baptised if we could get permission. There were another five guys who had got saved and wanted to go through the waters of Baptism. So I gave the Governor their names.

A week later while everyone else was locked up, our cell doors were opened and we were given a new towel and a new pair of underpants and told to go down to the bath-house. It was amazing, all the officers on duty at that time were Christians!

We had tried our best to keep it secret, but everyone knew. As we tried to tiptoe down the landing, guys started to bang their doors and shout things out. "Packie walks on water!" My face was turning bright red by this time, and we all were practically running now just to get out of the wing and away from all the banter. The whole gaol knew what was happening—it was the talk for days.

Down in the bath-house we filled a bath up with lukewarm water. We were a little nervous by it all; really none of us prisoners knew what to do, so I said "Just follow me guys, do whatever I do." I climbed into the bath, and was told by the minister to slide up until my knees were almost touching the huge taps. After making a confession of faith to the minister, (who had been invited into the prison to conduct this baptismal service) he prayed as he bent me backwards under the water and lifted me up again. It was fantastic! Everyone was laughing and smiling, even the governor ('*highly* irregular').

All five other candidates followed me, and the last guy happened to be a big guy called Geordie —and he was massive. When Geordie climbed in and lay back the water just rushed up the sides of the bath and soaked everybody standing at the side watching. Every one of them looked at the governor to see his reaction; the front of his suit was dripping wet. The governor looked down at his jacket, turned to look at the guy's jacket standing beside him and then he burst out laughing. Only then did the others feel free to join in too.

After they refilled the bath Big Geordie eventually got baptised too.

So it's on official record, as far as I am aware, that the first baptismal service in Belfast Prison was on the 29th of May 1981. I know others have taken place since but not officially; it's usually the inmates who do it by themselves, without any official involvement.

CHAPTER TWELVE

FACING THE FACTS

For every young Christian there is always a crisis that seems to follow conversion. The Devil will try everything to bring you back to himself. He knows where to hit to hurt you, and where it will hurt the most. He hit me hard, and I mean hard!

I wasn't long a Christian when I found out that my wife who continued to visit me every two weeks actually had another man living in our home with her. This was a terrible shock to me. I could not believe it, especially as she was still coming up to visit me each week. The friend who told me thought I already knew about this because apparently the other man moved into my home a few months before. This is the biggest fear for any married man in prison. What I had always feared was happening to me!

The next eight months I tried everything to try to save my marriage but to no avail. During that period there were times I got my hopes up only to see them dashed again. Once I got a letter suggesting we could make a go of it. I was so happy when I read this, but it was short-lived.

The final straw came for me when I was moved up to a new cell on the top landing. From there, out of the cell window, you can look down to the street and watch people coming in and out of the prison. I could wave to my family and friends as they were getting into their cars. It was the first visit with my wife since moving cells; we sat and held hands and kissed throughout the visit. Afterwards, I intended to surprise her by shouting from my cell window and waving to her as she crossed the road to go home. I rushed back to my cell, climbed up and waited for her to leave the prison.

After a few minutes I saw her crossing the road and walking towards her car. As I took a deep breath to shout, her car door opened and a man got out and he kissed her. My legs started to shake; my stomach knotted; I felt as if I had been gutted as I watched them drive away. While my wife had been sitting holding my hand across the table telling me how much she loved me, outside the prison another man was sitting waiting to take her home. She had told me she had finished with this man a month ago and wanted to save our marriage and I was so happy. But when with my own eyes I saw them together, I knew it was all lies; nothing had changed in their relationship. That day I knew my marriage was over, it was now only a dream. I had to accept the hard facts: I no longer had a wife; furthermore I had lost my son who was calling another man Daddy. During an earlier visit he actually said to me I have two daddies now and I realised then what the child had meant. I had no home to go back to. I found it hard to sleep and—worse— when I did, it was only to wake up with this terrible gut feeling of loneliness. It was hard to hide the pain, and yet I knew God would have to do something inside of me. I couldn't really share my hurt with anyone, I tried to, with a few other Christians, but they couldn't really understand what was happening. They all came out with these 'holy, hollow *clichés',* "Praise God, you're better off without her," or "All things work for our good. Trust God." I realised they meant good OK, but that wasn't what I wanted to hear. It wasn't healing the hurt in my heart. I needed someone to put their arm around me and just be a shoulder to cry on.

Sadly you don't find such people in prison. I only had God to turn to, but at times I felt my prayers stopped at the ceiling. This time of depression lasted almost a year. Not being loved, I realised, is not loneliness, because my family loved me and wrote letters to me; rather loneliness is not having someone to love, to care for.

It is in all of us, the need to be needed, to be wanted and loved by others. I continued to pray and ask God to heal my heart and to remove the love I still had for my wife. Eventually with much prayer and fasting I filed for a divorce, after having read everything in the Bible about the subject. Again I got mixed reactions from some of my Christian friends in prison. Some said divorce was a sin, period. Others pointed out that God divorced the Northern Kingdom of Israel for her adulterous ways. All I knew was that I did not want a divorce but that's what happened—it was part of the sentence. It didn't get any easier after that, God still had much to do to make my healing complete. I knew he would have to do something inside of me to relieve my broken heart. I just had to trust and leave everything with him.

The Devil didn't let up on me either. The hardest test of all was when this man and my wife had a row; in anger he lifted my three year-old son, put him up against a wall and punched him in the face. My son went into hospital and had an operation on his nose, but the bone structure was completely shattered and my son had to wait for the bone to develop before they could fix it. He developed a stutter and sometimes he would wake up screaming in the middle of the night because he couldn't breath. It was my sister who told me what had happened to my boy.

I couldn't believe this! Who would want to do such a thing to a small child?

I was very upset and angry, mostly at myself, for not being there to protect my son. I began to pray about this man, and I told God if he came into gaol I would stop being a Christian and kill him; he didn't deserve to live.

Anytime he came into my mind I would pray, "God keep him out of gaol, out of my way."

It was three years later when I got out on parole; everyone who knew the story told me not to go near my ex-wife (by this time she was living with someone else) or to go looking for this man. I didn't have any plans, but I wanted to see my boy, which I did, but I never saw this particular man. I wasn't worried about it; I knew I would eventually meet him, but I didn't expect to meet him so soon in the way that I did!

My parole ended and I went back into prison, I walked up and put my brown paper bag on top of my bed, lifted my cup and turned to go out and get some hot water for a cup of tea. I saw a man on the other landing looking over at me. It was him! He had come into gaol during the time I went home on parole. My heart started to beat faster. He immediately pulled his cell door closed, which automatically locks it. He stayed locked and refused to come out.

I knew he would have to come out some time and I would be ready for him when he did.

A few days later I was cutting the grass at the prison hospital. I was standing at the path and happened to look up and saw this man walking towards me; escorted by an officer over to the hospital. When he saw me he stopped and then walked around to the other side of the officer, who was now between us. When he came to where I was, I said to him " Have you punched any babies lately?"

He replied, "It was an accident."

"I am going to kill you," I answered.

The officer told him to keep on walking and just stared at me. There was a guy working along with me and he couldn't believe what I had just said to this man.

"You are a Christian and you just said you are going to kill that man."

"You don't know what he did to my baby" was my answer to him.

During lock-up after lunch I would usually read my Bible and pray. I would look out the hatch of my door to see if he came out for exercise. For a few weeks he remained locked, but then one day he decided to go outside. I watched as he walked downstairs. I decided to prepare myself, began to walk up and down my cell. I wanted to get rid of my other emotions, to feel nothing, only the desire to kill this man. I knew the yard was the best place to do what I had planned; I had to block out everything else and not worry about an officer seeing me. There was a distraction I had organised for this event to draw the guards away. If all went according to plan, it would be all over in a few moments; a body would be lying in the yard and the sirens would go off. There was little possibility of my being caught, I saw it happen before and no one was charged with the murder.

I was walking up and down waiting for the door to open, and waiting for the urge to rise up inside me to kill him. I was finding it hard—I couldn't seem to do it; there was no evil in me; I was struggling and feeling frustration. It was then God spoke to me in my mind, "David, forgive him."

I answered back "I'll forgive him after I've killed him," and I kept walking. Again it happened that I had this thought, "David forgive him," so I said, "I will not kill him, but I want to beat him badly, for it's only right to do this; he deserves it."

I wanted to make a deal with God, and God didn't want to know. All I could hear was "David forgive him." So I got angry with God, stopped walking, looked up and shouted, "Look what he did to my son!"

It was then God spoke to me again and said, "Look what they did to my Son!"

I fell to my knees and wept and I asked God to help me forgive him. I came up from my knees a different man, I went out into the yard where I saw him standing under the shelter. He was afraid—he reminded me of a scared rabbit caught in car headlights. As I walked towards him he did not move. I stopped just a few feet from him, looked into his eyes and saw the fear. I could easily have taken his life at that moment. Instead I said, "I am a Christian now; God has forgiven me and I forgive you for what you did to my son. You can stay in the yard, no one will harm you".

I walked back inside to my cell and lay down, I couldn't believe what I had just done.

A few days later my mother was up to see me, and I was called at the same time as this man for his visit. On our way down to the visiting area we had to go together through an "air lock" (you go through a steel gate and you are locked in; you walk to the other end and a guard opens another gate to let you pass through). The moment we were locked in this area he assumed I would attack him and he squatted down onto the floor trying to cover his face with his hands.

I told him to get up "I told you I would forgive you. I am not going to touch you." I turned and walked away.

As I sat talking to my mother I saw his mother get up and come across to my table. I stood up to meet her, and she actually put her arms around me and thanked me for forgiving her son. I didn't know what to reply to her so I said, "I am a Christian now" she smiled and went back to her seat. Later on back in cell I was lying on my bed thinking about what had happened. I still found it hard to believe I actually let him go, I had stabbed other people for less, I had beaten other guys with hammers for less. As I lay there, suddenly a thought ran across my mind, it was this: *I REALLY am a Christian. I REALLY am a Christian!*

Where did the evil go from within me? Who took it away? - GOD!

Where did the forgiveness come from ? Who gave me this? - GOD!

It was God!!

That day was a turning point in my life. I knew then I would never go back to my old life, or back to the Organisation again. I would never hold a gun or plant another bomb as long as I would live. From that day on I have never doubted my salvation because I know the power of God to change a person. As the old hymn says,

> The vilest offender who truly believes,
> that moment from Jesus a pardon receives!

I like the way the Bible puts it in 2 Corinthians 5 verse 17 "If any man be in Christ he is a new creature: old things are passed away; behold, ALL things are become new."

This is the power of the Gospel of Jesus Christ! Glory to God.

CHAPTER THIRTEEN

PACKIE THE PREACHER

"*I*t's all right for these guys coming in here telling us how God can change our lives; they go back out again. If I was going with them I'd be smiling too."

I was sitting directly behind the guy who made this comment during the Methodist service in church one thursday afternoon. I thought, *It's difficult to get any message across to these men because they cannot relate to them, so no one gives a thought to what they have to say.*

The thought came into my mind, *They would listen to me, because I don't get to go home afterwards, I also go back to my cell.* Perhaps I should talk to them and share my own experience of how my life has changed since becoming a Christian a few months earlier.

For some reason this thought remained with me, several times over the next week, *You speak to them.* I laughed to myself, *No way—I'd make a complete fool of myself.* Anyway the boys would give me a death; they would be shouting out things, maybe even throw the hymnbooks at me. I could not see myself standing up in front speaking to all these guys. Yet the thought still stayed with me.

It continued for another week, then I had another thought, *Maybe this is God talking to me*. I had heard many Christians say things like "Then God said to me . . . " I always wondered how they knew it was God speaking to them. How does God speak to people? Is it an audible voice, or what? Now I was a little confused: was this God telling me to do this? (maybe for me being Irish it takes things a little longer to reach the brain) *What if it is God? Man, that means I have to do it!* Now I was a nervous wreck.

I decided I would have to fast to check it out, and if it was God's idea he would have to get the prison chaplain to agree to it. That would be one way of proving it; he would have to allow me to get up to talk. As far as I was aware, no other prisoner had ever done this before.

The chaplain would be taking a chance: he wouldn't know what I would do. When I told him what was on my mind he asked me what I planned to say to them. I really didn't know.

"I just want to tell them that God has changed my life," that was all I could tell him. I was sort of expecting him to say "No, maybe some other time" but when he said "OK, in a fortnight's time you can speak on the Sunday morning," I almost died! Now I had really done it; he had said yes! Oh No!

The next two weeks were the longest I spent in gaol! I fasted for three days during that first week seeking God to give me the words to speak. The next week I did the same again, I prayed and asked God to confirm it as well by letting someone get converted by my testimony—that was the only thing I wanted in return. It had been announced the Sunday before that the speaker for the following week would be a Mr David Hamilton coming all the way from D Wing. Of course it was the talk of the gaol. Guys were shouting things at me all week like, "Packie, will you be dressing up like Batman on Sunday morning?", or, "You're only doing this so you can get at the wine in the minister's room." It was never said in a hostile way always as a laugh. But, man, was I nervous!

Finally Sunday came around, I have never seen the church as full, and some of the guys there hadn't been in church since they were christened as babies! I was out in the back room with the Rev. David Jardine—he wanted us to pray before the service began. I remember him asking me, "Are you all set? have you got your notes ready?"

"No, I don't have any."

"What are you going to say to them? " was his next question.

I looked at him with a slight smile, or perhaps it was more of a nervous gesture than anything else and said, "I don't know, but God knows." I think I saw the same look on his own face before he said, "Let's go out and join the others."

I tried to avoid making eye contact with anyone; I found it hard to sing the hymns and I could sense everyone looking at me. Occasionally I would glance quickly over all the faces in the congregation, and immediately regret doing so.

It seemed like the service had gone on for four hours, and yet before I knew it, it was my turn next, when the minister said, "Our speaker needs no introduction today. Most of you know him, it's David Hamilton, all the way from D Wing." The whole place erupted with shouts and whistles; my face was as red as a beetroot; I just stood there motionless, waiting for it to die down, Many times I had taken part in this very thing. Now here I was at the receiving end. Now I knew how some of those speakers must have felt.

After a minute the place settled, and I began to talk to them. One guy who was a well-known leader of a terrorist group, shouted out, "Packie, you haven't repented of everything you did." Again there was an outburst of laughter,

"Maybe not to the police, but to God I have, so that's enough for me!" I shouted back. Again everyone laughed—I now was beginning to relax; it seemed all the nervousness I had just a few minutes before was completely gone, It was replaced with boldness and a confidence. Now I had no fear at all. I began just to tell them the truth that my life was completely changed since I had asked Jesus to take charge of my life a year before. I told them it was the best year of my life (that got quite a few laughs) and yet in another way it was also the hardest year of my life. Some of them who were my friends outside were aware of my domestic problems—at that particular time I was still praying for reconciliation to take place with my wife. I told them that through it all I had someone who stuck closer to me than a friend, and that he was interested as much in them as he was in me. That person was the Lord Jesus Christ.

It seemed the bolder I got the quieter they got! I knew God was moving amongst them by the power of the Holy Spirit. That day was a turning point in my life. From then on, the only desire I had was to tell people that Jesus loved them and could change their lives as he changed mine. Nothing excites me as much, even today, I still feel exactly the same, I have no real care for anything else, Before that day, I would have said I was introverted, timid in the fear of making a fool of myself. I hadn't any great education, so I had no confidence in doing something outside the group, I had what is known as a "gang-set mentality" yet that day I realised I had stepped out from it and had begun to stand alone. I was making my own decisions now.

Afterwards I talked with the Chaplain he told me he couldn't believe how long I had spoken for, and without the use of any notes. I knew God had anointed me; it was as if he had taken over and put the words in my mouth, as he promises in his word.

What I didn't know then was that the anointing that day would be confirmed to me not so far in the future, and that I would become an evangelist and that would be my work full-time.

Neither the chaplain or I could have imagined then that event would be the first of many times when we would share the platform together. Nor would it be confined to just this particular prison, or indeed to Northern Ireland, but that we would find ourselves doing the same thing again in prisons and churches around New York, U.S.A!

The next few days following the service I was waiting to hear if anyone had made a decision to follow Christ. Thursday came—still nothing. I went to the Methodist service that afternoon. When the minister, Robert Russell (in prison there was a chaplain for each of the four main denominations; Presbyterian, Anglican, Methodist and Roman Catholic) got up to preach he said I want to tell you men something that happened on Sunday night past. He went on to say how he had challenged his congregation that evening by telling them that a young man who got converted in the prison a year before, was the preacher that morning in the gaol, standing up to witness before all those men how God had changed his life. "That takes guts! how many of you could do it?" he asked "How many of you are willing to stand up now and acknowledge you need God in your life?"

He followed on by saying, that it was only a few moments later that an old lady stood up and made her way out to the centre aisle and slowly walked to the front of the church. She told him she had been coming to church sixty years and never once had made a commitment of her life to Christ. She said, "That young man even though he's in prison has something in his life that I lack. I want to know God in the way that he does." When I heard this I couldn't stop the tears from flowing. Someone had got saved from hearing my testimony, but not in the way I expected: not a prisoner, but an old lady over seventy years old.

Later on, I made a vow to God that I would never speak to a stranger for more than three minutes without telling him how God had changed my life. I have sought to live by that same vow for the past seventeen years now. And do you know something else? It still excites me even now when I share the Gospel—it's the greatest message known to man.

CHAPTER FOURTEEN

PRISON FELLOWSHIP

It was around this time I first was introduced to a man called James McIlroy. He came into the prison to sing and I found out he was the director of a Christian organisation called Prison Fellowship, which had recently started to work in the prisons of Northern Ireland. Although the work was fairly new in Ireland, it was already working in many other countries worldwide. It was founded by a man called Charles Colson, who was former special counsel to President Richard Nixon, and had spent seven months in prison for Watergate-related offences.

It was upon his release from prison that this ministry was birthed in his heart. Today, it is an international prison outreach and Chuck Colson is an international respected author and speaker. His books include *Born Again*, and *Life Sentence*, both of which I read while in prison. I never imagined then that years later, my own story would be included in one of his books, or that Chuck himself would come to visit me in Belfast prison.

James McIlroy became a regular figure around the prison, visiting men not only in "The Crumlin" but in other prisons in Northern Ireland as well. At first I didn't know how to accept him. Like many guys I was suspicious of him, one of these do-gooders. As time went by, I would hear guys talking about him, "He's OK". One guy told me he asked him to collect the money from the gate to go buy a present for his wife, and he did! That impressed me, not too many would go out of their way to go shopping for a prisoner's wife. Word soon got around he was for real; prisoners have a way of knowing who is genuine and who isn't. If there was a need that a prisoner had, James would try to help as long as it didn't break any of the prison rules. On one occasion a prisoner's wife couldn't get up to the prison to visit because of transport problems: James McIlroy solved the problem by driving her up to the prison, not just the once but for the next four years! Each week he would collect this woman and sometimes children too, drive them up to the prison and then sit outside and wait to take them home again. He never once accepted money offered towards his petrol costs.

I began to like this man and over the next few years we became good friends. I started to look forward to when he was due to take part in the prison service. Sometimes he would sing, but I forgave him because we were friends. He was a trained singer—whatever that meant—and his singing seemed popular to a lot of folk, but to me, well, I have good taste in music, like Bob Dylan or Van Morrison. James' singing is a long-standing joke between us. He even threatened to sing at my second wedding: I had to pay him not to!

James asked me to work with him in Prison Fellowship a year before my release; I said I would pray about it. Afterwards I told him I would, as long as he promised not to sing. He said, "OK, but if you step out of line, I will!"

For the two years before my release I worked up in the prison garden. My job was cutting the grass, which took me all over the prison. We had a prison graveyard, where prisoners who were hanged got buried. It was a patch of land behind the prison hospital, alongside the high stone wall, which was used by the dog handlers as a run to exercise their dogs in. It was always a gloomy place to work; it seemed the sun never reached into this particular corner. There was nothing to suggest it was actually a cemetery. The nearest clue to be found was on the cold stone wall, where at eye level one could see etched out on one of the stones a name and a date. That was all and even this was crudely done so that one would think it to be no different from a thousand other names to found scraped on the prison walls all around the place. But I knew the difference. Most men who etched their names out wrote their name and how long their sentence was, but for those buried there, it was just the date they were executed, and it was carved by someone else.

The only good thing about working in that little graveyard was the peace and quietness that I often experienced there. It was perhaps the only place in the whole gaol I could actually get to be alone with the Lord.

I have a Bible with around fifty autographs signed on the back pages, mostly signatures of men who were doing time with me or of special speakers. One of the special memories that is reflected by those autographs is that of the prison chaplain, Rev. Bill Vance. He had been off work for a long time recovering from major heart surgery, but returned one thursday night to lead our bible study group. I was pleased to see him and remained to talk to him after the others had left just for five minutes before lock-up.

He always had a smile, never once did I hear him complain or talk harshly about any one. If I complained about how I felt I had been mistreated by an officer, Bill would answer, "We should pray for him. We don't know what's going on in his life or what concerns are causing him to act that way."

That's what we would end up doing—praying. That night before I went to lock up, I asked him to sign my bible for me which he did. He wrote a reference as well which I couldn't stop to read then, for I could hear doors slamming shut and I was already late for lock up. So I said, "Have to run here, goodnight Bill." I remember he looked up with that familiar smile, and answered "Goodnight". He lifted his hand and waved as I ran out the door. The following morning I went down to my work, as soon as I walked in, an officer called me over and said, "I've some bad news for you David: the Rev. Vance died early this morning." I could hardly take it in, I was very upset, I found it hard to work and so the officer allowed me to go back to my cell. The first thing I did was to lift my bible and see what Bill had written the night before. His words pierced my heart:

> For I am persuaded, that neither death, nor life, nor angels nor principalities nor powers, nor things

present, nor things to come, nor height nor depth, nor any other created thing shall be able to separate us from the love of God, which is in Christ Jesus our Lord. (Romans 8:38)

I smiled to myself and thought, *Bill Vance was ready to go, he wasn't afraid to die, because he knew Jesus personally.* That's why he could write that precious text in my Bible.

Another is the signature of a prison officer. I have fond memories of. One day while working up the garden, I was standing at the wire fence talking to him. I knew him to be a fine Christian, he was probably the most respected officer in "the Crum", one of the P.T.I.'s, who worked in the gym. There were two officers who were responsible for all the physical fitness in the prison, and they were as different as chalk and cheese. The other guy liked to be seen as a tough guy—he was a big guy for sure who enjoyed getting the chance to beat prisoners up: he was on the riot squad and loved it!

I remembered him from the riot we had in "C" Wing a few years before. He was fond of a drink but if he got too much, we got no exercise in the gym, If he was working on the Saturday we never knew for certain if we would get a football match; if he had had the night out, then he would most probably forget about having a match. But Sam was totally the opposite; he would go out of his way to make sure the guys got their football, even to the extent of coming into work during his holidays.

Sam was up cutting the grass verge around the edge of the pitch using diesel to burn away the weeds. Between us was this seven metre high fence topped with razor wire. After we had talked for a while I turned to go back to my work and he turned around to carry on with his. I hadn't walked fifteen metres away when I heard a massive explosion behind me, and I turned around to see a huge black mushroom-shaped cloud rising upwards. As the smoke cleared; I could hardly believe my eyes! He was standing there burning in front of me; all of his clothes were burned off. I could not go to help him, I cursed that high fence and ran up to the office and shouted to the officer to sound the alarm. Before he lifted the phone the alarm sounded—the sound of the explosion had been heard all over the prison and naturally they all assumed it was a terrorist attack. I ran back to the fence were others prisoners were gathered watching the drama. By this time another officer was on hand and he was rolling "Jaunty" (that's what we called him) across the ground to put out the fire. Parts of his flesh were still burning. The officer was one of the dog handlers on patrol around the perimeter so he happened to be quite close by when the explosion happened and it was he that sounded the alarm. He immediately ran to his aid.

Later on we were told his heart stopped on the way to hospital. Apparently this happened three times, but they were able to bring him back, thanks to the medics. It was touch and go if he would live; he had multiple body burns. Of course all the men who were Christians were praying for his recovery, and many others besides, I was amazed how many other prisoners said to me , "Don't forget to pray for Jaunty" I was as much amazed as the authorities were to find out that the tuck shop was sold out of "get well" cards, bought by prisoners to send to this officer. "Why," many officers were asking, "what made Sam so popular with the inmates?"

I asked a few guys why they had sent cards, some of whom were known as hard men and feared by many around the prison. Their answers were almost always the same.

"Because Jaunty is sound, he makes sure we get our football, He's OK"—that's about as high a compliment any officer will get as far as inmates are concerned. It's true, you know; Sam got as much abuse shouted at him as any other officer, but underneath they respected him and it was at such a time as this they let him know that. If you were to ask Sam about it all, he would just shrug and say, "I don't know, I am only doing my job"—so he was, but the way he did it showed he cared for men too, and we all knew that.

My life in Prison was anything but dull. Once I got caught smuggling, a very serious offence in gaol —you can get time added on to your sentence for this. Of course it depends on what one is smuggling: most times it likely to be drugs or weapons. But it wasn't any of these I was caught with.

I had just moved in to share a cell with "Big D". Many nights we would lay and sing choruses we had learnt in David Jardine's weekly Bible study. Sometimes we would forget some of the words but it never put us off, I remember thinking one night "It would be great if we had two hymnbooks. We could sing to our hearts' content. It wasn't long after there was a riot in another part of the prison; prisoners on remand took over their wing in protest. It was a few days before things got restored to normal, but by this time a lot of the furniture was broken up and used as weapons by inmates. What they didn't break, the guards did—each cell was stripped bare and everything tossed out on to the landing. All this rubbish was dumped in the garden to be eventually taken away to the city dump outside. There was a mountain of stuff, broken chairs, cupboards, beds, bookshelves etc., all lying in pieces. We were told by the officer in charge of us not to go near this part of the garden, it was off-limits.

A few days later that I was told to go empty a wheelbarrow of old cabbage foliage down in the dump. While I was down there I looked across at all this mountain of junk and noticed a pile of red books lying scattered around the ground. it was a pile of the prison hymnbooks, called "Redemption Hymnals". I immediately thought to myself, *if only I could get my hands on two of them*. So I made a plan, I started to rake up any debris I could find around the garden just to get me back down to the dump again, each time I made my way a little closer toward the junk pile.

By my fourth or fifth journey I worked up close enough to the pile to be in reach of the hymnbooks, I had to time it right when the guard was looking away. I reached over and grabbed two of the hymnbooks and stuffed them inside my overalls. Everything went according to plan, I was feeling good with myself. A few moments later, I was walking back up again. Suddenly there was a shout.

"Stop that prisoner!" A guard with a dog come running up towards us, he was panting out of breath,

"Get up against the wire and spread your arms and legs, NOW" he said; both he and his dog were snarling. He started to talk through his radio to the control room, "Prisoner apprehended, beginning to search, over." He turned to the other officer who was my escort and said "The security cameras up on the wall spotted him lifting something from the pile of junk and stuffing it inside his overalls. You should have been watching him more closely." The officer's face became very serious, "What was it?" he asked, he began to frisk me. Almost immediately he felt them. "Found something" he said, quite excited, into the radio.

"What is it?" the officer with me asked. I looked over my shoulder to see his face; he pulled out the two hymnbooks. Both guards looked at them in amazement, and the dog handler was red-faced as he spoke into the radio "It's, uh, two hymnbooks, over."

"Please repeat, over" was the immediate response from the control room. Again the officer said,

"It's two flaming hymnbooks!" He brought me up to the officer in charge of the garden party. In the office he said "The cameras caught Hamilton smuggling these." At that he tossed the two hymnbooks onto the table, "You deal with him, " and with that he turned and walked out.

"Auld Jaunty" (the officer in charge of the garden, who had the same surname as the one who was burned by accident) started to shout at me; a few moments later he stopped and said "No more of this, do you hear me, Hamilton?"

"I do, I am sorry about this."

"OK, now clear that table, it's time for tea. Call all the other men in." He turned and walked back into the small kitchen, I cleared the table as ordered, and lifted the hymnbooks again—didn't know where to put them— and stuck them down the back of my trousers again! I was able to get them back to my cell without being caught. That night we had a Holy Ghost party: we sang all night long. We sang every song with the same tune, if there were too many words we just skipped them and went on to the next line. We thought it was great. We were the only ones who thought that—every one else was up at their windows shouting at us to be quiet; we shouted back in between songs, "Any requests? Call them out!" They all thought we were mad. We got to keep them, even during cell searches. The guards let them remain.

Today, even now when I see one of those old Redemption hymnbooks it brings a smile to my face. I wonder if Paul and Silas had a Redemption hymnal when they sang all night in prison.

God proved himself more and more to me every passing day. he was interested in every aspect of my life. One incident that really proved this was through the handicrafts. I still was doing the leather work in partnership with my mate Big J, and one day we had a row: a man had ordered some items and promised to pay me the day he got released, I decided to trust him but he failed to come across with the money. Of course Big J was furious. He said it was my fault we had lost thirty pounds because I was a Christian now and trusted everybody and now we were being ripped off. He made a new rule from now on: no one gets anything unless they pay first, money up front! "No more trusting people, OK?"

"I cannot agree to that," I answered back. "As a Christian I want to look for the good in people not the bad, I want people to see I trust them."

"You and your trust . . . What about our thirty pounds?" he shouted back.

"Listen," I said, "you haven't lost any money, it's my loss, OK?"

"You're mad, Packie, since you have become a Christian, do you know that?"

I laughed, "Do you think so?" He shook his head and off he went.

As I was lying on my bed I thought about our conversation, and I said to the Lord, "I think it's right to trust people, I don't like this bit of saying I don't trust you so you must pay up front, Lord show me if I am doing the right thing".

He answered me in an unusual way.

It was a few days later, I got my weekly visit from my mother. During the course of our conversation she said to me, "David, something strange happened the other night, this man who lives near us, who is a Christian, called to our house on Friday night, and said, 'I know this may sound strange to you Mrs Hamilton, but I was praying earlier and this thought came into my head to give your son David thirty pounds, I believe it was God who told me to do this, so will you accept it please and leave in for him; tell him it's from the Lord.' "

I could not believe what I was hearing! "Mum, wait till you hear the story behind it," I said. She was amazed by it all.

Of course after my visit that day the first person I wanted to tell was my mate Big J. When I found him he was playing a game of snooker, so I called him over to tell him.

"Wait till you hear this, you will not believe it," I said; when I told him the whole story he just stood there motionless. At the end he said "Is that it? That would have been sixty pounds we would have had, if you hadn't have trusted your man."

He was completely blind to the fact that God had worked a miracle. The man who God used to replace the thirty pounds I had lost was Derek Jackson, an ex-terrorist who had been miraculously healed of cancer.

Derek began to visit me after that. He would write and send me in study books which helped me a lot in my early days. When I got out on my first parole he took me to my first Christian meeting on the outside. I have never seen this man without a smile on his face. He always seems to radiate the Lord. He was another of those special people that God sent alongside me to build me up in my own walk.

That experience helps me to believe God for miracles, to pray for miracles, and to see miracles take place. Another time I remember it was coming in to winter nights, and it was starting to get cold out in the exercise yard. I needed a jacket to keep me warm, so I prayed and asked the Lord to help me get a denim jacket, not a Wrangler, which were the most popular at that time, but instead I wanted a Levi jacket.

It was the following day a guy came into my cell and said, "My mother! I asked her to get me a denim jacket and send it in and what does she buy me? A Levi, and I told her a Wrangler. It's even the wrong size for me—it's too big. She cannot do anything right."

My curiosity was stirred, "What size is the jacket?" I asked,

"42" He answered. "Why, are you interested in buying it? It's going cheap."

He asked for six ounces of tobacco. I said "No, I'll give you ten, OK?" He couldn't believe his luck. I had loads of tobacco, always, so it was no problem to pay him.

I was thrilled to have a new Levi denim jacket so soon, and my friend was just as thrilled to get rid of it so quickly.

I knew it was God's provision in answer to prayer.

CHAPTER FIFTEEN

MAKING A STAND

Since my conversion almost a year before, I began to talk to everybody, regardless whether they were Loyalist or Republican, sex-offender or thief, Protestant or Catholic. It made no difference, especially to God.

This annoyed some folk, who got angry when they saw me talking to sex-offenders and others I would have fought with before my conversion. Now I was trying to befriend them.

I remember two IRA men whom I would speak to whenever I met them, though they never acknowledged me at any time and always looked away in disgust. This didn't bother me any—I knew it would take a long time for most of the guys to accept me as a genuine Christian, especially Catholics. A few of them did at this time, but not these particular two.

It happened one day I was sitting outside in the exercise yard alone, reading my Bible, and these two guys were out walking around the yard. They had passed me a number of times but still up to that point had never talked to me. It was quite a surprise to me when one of them as he passed me by set a sweet on top of my Bible! I looked up as they walked on by, and when they came around again I said, "Thanks, I hope it's not poisoned." They laughed and stopped walking and one of them began to speak to me, and said, "I've been watching you to see if you really are one of these born-again Christians."

"So what's your conclusion then?" I asked him,

"We think you're genuine; every time we see you, you're reading your Bible, you really do believe all that stuff," he said as he pointed to my Bible. That day was a turning point with them guys; they always spoke to me from then on.

I had another experience with an IRA man about two years later and I remember it well. That particular morning I was waiting to go out on my first parole home. This was my first three-day leave and that morning I was sitting in my cell with the cell door open waiting to be called. I looked up and was surprised when an IRA man came walking into my cell.

"You must be the happiest man in this prison. Every time I see you, you have a smile on your face, Is it because you're a Christian, or what is it?" he asked.

"You're right first time, Sean: that's what it is. It's because I know Jesus Christ personally," I answered with a smile on my face.

"Is it OK to sit down?" he asked (he knew it's not the done thing, Protestant having a Catholic, or vice versa, in one's cell).

"It's no problem," I answered. "Sit down man."

He went on, "How can you say, Packie, you know Jesus, like—personally. No one can say that, not even the priest."

"Listen," I said, "you can, if you really want to. What I have, you can have also. Then you can know Him for yourself, that's what the Bible teaches us." I opened my Bible up to show him, and we talked for quite a while, he asking the questions and me trying to answer them. Then he said to me, "I would really love to have what you have Packie."

"Sean," I replied, "you can have what I have, simply by asking Jesus to take your life over from today, it's that simple."

"But how?" he asked. I could see on his face he was really searching, he really wanted to know. I said to him, "If you want your life changed then repeat this prayer, after me and make it your own prayer."

As I said the prayer out loud, he repeated it word for word; when I finished it, he looked up at me, his face was beaming, his eyes shining. We were both laughing.

When I got out of prison the first thing I did was to go and buy a Bible for Sean. If someone had said on my first day back out of prison that's what I would do, I would have gone mad. Me! Buy a Bible for an IRA man? It sounds so far from reality I never could have imagined such a thing happening. But it did!

(I have included this prayer at the end of this book, if you would like to know Jesus Christ personally, then turn to it now and pray it out aloud, and let God change your life today. Today can be the first day of the rest of your life not just a new start in life, but rather a new life to start from this day on)

Occasionally there are times when it is difficult as a Christian and you have to make a stand. I guess one of my hardest trials was during a prison riot.

Prison riots never really achieve anything. I had been involved in my fair share of them over the years, but it's worse when you're a Christian and there is one planned to come down, and you're stuck in the middle of it.

That's just what happened, I was sitting in the dining hall having my lunch, when the guy sitting next to me said, "Don't get up from your chair, there is a protest planned, it's a sit down, no one moves." I knew the rules OK. No one is allowed to get up and leave and if they do, how do you stop them? There are thieves, muggers, rapists, all kinds of guys in for all kinds of crimes; how do you stop them from leaving?

It's simple—someone came up with this idea: the first person who gets up to leave pays the price for everyone who wants to go. If a man moves from his table then the rule is that everyone throws their steel tray at him, which leaves him in a mess, cut to pieces. Being bombarded by maybe a hundred steel trays is not a pretty sight. Only then are others free to leave, but the first is the sacrifice. No-one wants to be the first.

I sat there, thinking about all this: *This is all I need, how can I say I'm a Christian yet take part in a protest, this will destroy my witness, all the guards will say you're still a paramilitary when you obey their orders.* I started to pray, "Lord show me what you want me to do." I had no sooner prayed this in my mind, than suddenly I felt as if an unseen hand had taken hold of my collar and lifted me up out of my seat! I could not believe this was actually happening to me. Here I was walking through all these tables towards the door, waiting for the trays to start flying! As I walked past the centre tables where all the top men sat, unofficially, but it was here that most decisions were made by the paramilitaries, I looked over at these men.

One of them spoke out, " It's not because Packie's afraid that he's walking out, but it's because he is a Christian." No-one moved; I continued walking toward the doors; I could see the riot squad standing alert ready for the order to rush in once the doors opened. I kept walking. I couldn't understand it. Why was nothing happening?! My heart was still pounding. *What's stopping them,* I thought! *Seconds seem like hours, any second now they will all throw their trays*...I was wrong, they never did, and I walked out the doors. Immediately others who were waiting for the chance to run, jumped up because they knew I was the scapegoat, so they were free to go. In a matter of minutes the whole protest was over and everyone continued to leave the dining hall. It was over as quick as it started.

Back in my cell, I lay on the bed looking up at the ceiling, "God don't do that again! It's not good for my health," I shouted.

But I knew he protected me, while one hand lifted me up the other was around me keeping me safe. I knew that was one experience I wouldn't forget in a hurry.

Two years later, one afternoon when I was working up in the prison garden, a short-termer (a prisoner serving a sentence under two years) asked me a question: "Packie did you ever stop a riot in the gaol?" I was surprised by this question and asked him why he would ask me such a question. He said that during the lunch-time lock-up, two officers were standing idle, outside his cell-door, talking.

The conversation was overheard by this prisoner. One of them said, "Packie is not afraid to stand up as a Christian—remember when he stopped the riot in D Wing? He wouldn't have risked his life like that if he wasn't for real."

I laughed, even the Screws remembered.

Another time when I did something out of the ordinary was when I was working as an orderly in the dining hall serving out the food. It happened that four men just came on to the wing that day after being sentenced for their involvement in a sex-scandal which involved a boys' home in Belfast. It got a lot of media coverage, and lots of people were angry about it.

These four men were sitting at a table in the dining hall when everyone got out for tea. They were getting all these dirty looks from everyone, and it was obvious they were frightened and afraid to move. As I was watching them I realised although they each had a dinner none of them had cutlery to eat it with. I was working behind the wire grill, so I walked over to the sink and got knives, forks and spoons for all of them. I then went to pass them through the wire to another prisoner and I asked him to pass them over to them, he looked at me and said,

"You must be joking! they would all kill me." He meant the other men there in the dining hall. So I turned to the guard and said, "Open the grill, and let me out." I then walked over to their table and give each of them a set of cutlery. Everyone was watching, and then they all started to hiss at me. I got really angry and turned around and shouted, "These men are entitled to have a knife fork and spoon, just like the rest of you. I don't expect you to eat your diner with your fingers nor them either!"

I walked back to the grill and the screw hurriedly let me back in; he didn't know what to expect.

It was amazing out of all the men there, only one man pulled me up later about it. There was plenty of guys there who could easily have pulled my head off and thought nothing about it. That evening this particular guy came over to me and said he didn't like what I had done. He was looking for a reaction from me. I wasn't afraid, just smiled at him. He was a Catholic guy and I knew he didn't really want trouble. He was trying to act tough, waiting to see what I would do. I answered him by saying, "Jimmy I didn't do it to win favour-of-the-month award, neither does it bother me what you or anybody else think about what I do; I try to do what I think is right. If you want to make something more out of it, it's up to you, man"

He was unsure about it, so he decided to let it drop at that, he just gave a shrug, turned and walked away. I was glad nothing more came of it.

I never thought I would see the day I would risk my life to help sex-offenders, looking back afterwards I said to myself, "Man, I've come along way from wanting to burn them in the exercise yard! The truth was I didn't see them now as any different from the rest of us, or any worse for that matter. None of us were better than anybody else, we all have broken the law—both man's and God's—and now we were all paying for it.

Some of the things that happened to me while in prison I know some people would find it hard to believe. I used to have a tattoo of the word "SEX" in the middle of my right hand. As I was washing myself in the sink and throwing water over my face, I pulled out the plug and as the water began to twist down the plug, I saw a word in the water turning round and round. I read the word SEX!

I immediately looked at my hand and my tattoo was gone. I turned to the guy beside me and said my tattoo just washed down the sink, He just turned and said it must have been one of those rub-on ones. He just laughed and didn't believe me. I said to myself *If you tell anyone else they will say you're mad.* I only shared that with a few people and they laughed too. I learned there are some times things happen that are better left untold.

The tattoo cleansing was one of many miracles, that God has given me since he saved me from a wretched life. But the gift of Salvation I know now to be the greatest miracle of all!

After I had served three years I was eligible for my first home leave, I had applied for it and was waiting to hear if it was granted.

It was on Christmas Eve that the No.1 governor decided to see me (there are governors for each wing). I had been a Christian for over a year at that time and

I hadn't been in any trouble since my conversion. I was surprised when told he wanted to see me. For one thing I hadn't expected to be called out into his own personal office. Standing in front of his desk, I looked at this man, the No.1 gov. He was soon to retire—the sooner the better, some said. He had a bad reputation from staff and prisoners alike, and I was soon to find the reason for this myself.

He looked up from reading my file and said, "Hamilton, your record in prison is excellent, you have been a good prisoner, It seems you work well in the kitchen and are studying to be a cook."

I smiled at him and answered, "Yes, Sir." I thought to myself, *I am getting out on home leave here ...*

The governor did not smile back but went on to say, "I also have been reading your police record from outside. It's atrocious, and as far as I am concerned you haven't changed any. You are not getting home leave—Out you go."

Our interview ended just as quick as that. I couldn't believe it. I was still standing looking at him, until the officer gave me a tug indicating for me to follow him out.

The thought in my mind was " ...Haven't changed any?" *If only you knew, Governor. At least God knows and I know that I am a changed man—that's the important thing.* It was a big disappointment for me not getting that Christmas leave.

CHAPTER SIXTEEN

CALLED TO THE MINISTRY

I had begun to study in prison, for a few reasons, it was a good way to help pass the time and also to try and get a proper education, something I hadn't taken seriously before.

I tried to complete one course each year I was in prison. In my final year I studied for an A-Level course in religious studies. I was to sit the exam three months before my release. Because my mind was on passing this exam, it kept me from getting gate fever. I was glad when I got the result to say I'd passed it, my first A-Level.

One day we were kept locked up because an officer had been murdered. As I was praying and reading my Bible that morning, I read something that seemed to jump out of the pages at me, it was Acts 26:16-18.

But rise, and stand upon thy feet; for I have appeared unto thee for this purpose, to make thee a minister and a witness both of these things which thou has seen, and of those things in which I will appear unto thee; delivering thee from the people, and from the

Gentiles, unto whom now I send thee, to open their
eyes, and to turn them from darkness to light, and
from the power of Satan unto God, that they may
receive forgiveness of sins, and inheritance among
them which are sanctified by faith that is in me.

Even when I tried to carry on reading I kept feeling
prompted to go back and read these verses over again.
I realised that God was speaking to me. This was a
personal commission—what God wanted of me. I
remember the date well, it was the 16th of February
82, The actual meaning puzzled me; did it really mean
" a minister and a witness"? The witness part was OK
for me, but this minister bit...What did God mean? A
minister, like Batman? No way, man; it couldn't be! I
searched all the Bible commentaries I could find, but
none gave me any real explanation.

It was only two days later when I learned the truth.
I went to the Methodist service, where we were having
a guest speaker that afternoon. His name was the Rev
Derek Haskins and I remember as he got up to speak,
he held up three pages of pink paper:

"This is my sermon, that I had planned to speak,
but I am not going to preach it, you will be glad to
know. Instead I feel God wants me to tell you how I
became a minister."

He went on to tell us how he had only a normal
education, had left school early and started working
in the shipyard in Belfast. It was there God called him
out to go into full time ministry.

That afternoon I listened as this man answered
every question that I had asked God just the few days
before. I kept telling God all the reasons why I
couldn't really be a minister, now I was listening to

God telling me through this man, "You shall be!" If God says it then that's enough. I knew then deep down in my heart, that God had a plan for my life, that I was called as a minister of the Gospel. A warm, peaceful feeling engulfed my heart.

I never would have considered it possible, never had such a thought even entered my head. It was far beyond me. But I thank God for it; there is no greater calling, no other profession, no other ambition that could satisfy me more. Nothing thrills me more than to be called into the ministry to serve my Lord Jesus Christ.

I knew that day I would not be going back to my trade ever again. But I didn't know what I would actually do upon my release. This is how God revealed his will for me to work for Prison Fellowship:

Time began to go in faster, it seemed. I eventually came down to my last year. My father began asking me "What do you plan to do, workwise, when you get released for good?" All I could say was, "I don't know yet, Dad. God hasn't shown me yet." He didn't know what to say in answer to this. Every visit he would ask the same question and I would answer, "I am still praying for God to show me".

Poor Dad he was doing everything in his power not to blow up on the visit!

A little time later, when I'd about eight months left to serve, I had been talking to the prison chaplain, Rev. David Jardine. He told me he was praying about my release and what I should do afterwards in the way of work. He told me he was on the Executive Board of Prison Fellowship and felt I should consider working along with James McIlroy. I smiled at that. By this time I knew James a lot better, we had talked a few times but I hadn't thought about us working together.

"I will certainly pray about this and see what the Lord says to me about it" I said. That night I did just that. I asked the Lord to show me a sign, if this was his doing. As I read my Bible later on that evening, my attention was drawn to this verse: "I have opened a door for you no man can shut." My heart leaped, this is what I wanted to know. "Lord, can you give me another sign, just to confirm it?"

The following day I was working up in the garden cutting the grass, It was a good day and the afternoon sun was shining. I heard my name called "Hamilton visit. " Now that was a surprise! I looked up to see an officer waiting to escort me back with him over to the main building, "You have an ecclesiastical visit," he shouted.

As I walked down the hill towards the main building, I felt something within me say, *This day is a day you are going to remember.* I didn't know who it was that wanted to see me and it was a real surprise to see James McIlroy when I walked through the door into the visit cubicle.

After a few moments of general talk, James told me he had been at a meeting the night before and a Roman Catholic nun spoke to him and said "It would be better if there were an ex-prisoner who could work alongside you."

As he travelled the long drive home that night, he said it seemed the words the nun spoke echoed around his ears, and it was my name and face he kept seeing before him. It touched him that much and he decided to come and see me the very next day.

When he finished telling all this I laughed "I supposed you were talking to David Jardine too?" I said, knowing what I thought to be the answer.

"No" he said, "Why do ask that?"

When he said no, I was shocked. I then told him what had happened the day before and how David had offered me the same job. Now it was his turn to be shocked!

We both knew then this was God's doing. I said "Let me pray about this" (as if I needed to). It seemed to be the only thing to say. But I knew inside me this was God's doing. That night I couldn't wait to be in my cell alone, just to get talking to the Lord. After praying I started to read the Bible, and as usual God spoke to me through what I read " I went unto Troas to preach the Gospel, and found a door opened unto me... " I just shouted "Praise God! Thank you Jesus!" and that was that. I knew the next step, that's all I needed to know. At last I knew what God wanted me to do once released.

I remember thinking, *That will please my Dad just to get an answer on our next visit.*

As I hadn't much time left to serve, I had started to pray about my relationship with James McIlroy. Every day I prayed that I would be accepted by his family, James and I got on the best; many times I wondered about his wife, *Maybe she will have problems with me as an ex-prisoner.* James had said to me, "On your parole you can come and stay in my home in Randalstown." I just smiled, I was still worried how his wife would find me—an ex-con.

I remember meeting Margaret for the first time. She seemed very warm and friendly toward me, a beautiful lady, who seemed to have no qualms about having ex-prisoners, staying in her home. It soon became obvious to me Margaret was behind her husband in all that he did.

She even asked me if I wanted a hot water bottle for bed! I laughed and said no thanks. She then told me to try not to waken her mum who slept in the room directly below my room and not to drop my shoes on the floor when I took them off. Although they were nursing her mother, they still had an open house and everyone was welcomed there.

I liked that. I really felt accepted in James's home, and with his family too.

Later on as I got to know them better I found all of his sons and daughters were great, especially the twin girls, and were fully behind their dad in his work. The reason for this was that they each had a personal relationship with the Lord and they were a strong Christian family, the first Christian family I'd ever met. They had no suspicions toward me but readily accepted me from that first night on and we all became good friends. I lay in bed laughing to myself that night in James's house. I had no need to feel nervous. I knew God had answered all my prayers about this family.

My next parole didn't go according to plans. I was planning to go out to attend a Prison Fellowship world conference and spend the weekend with Charles Colson. It so happened a week before I was with an officer working up the garden, I remember it started to pour out of the heavens, torrents of rain. I had been working down on my knees planting rose buds, so we ran for cover underneath a doorway. It was then this officer said to me, "Why have you stopped working? Go back out and carry on, I will stand here and watch you." I looked at him to see if he was joking—He wasn't.

"Mister, I will get pneumonia if I go out in that rain to work" I replied.

He just said "You will get wet, not me. Now get back to work."

I got angry and saw red, "Is that right, well I've news for you: I won't get wet either, because I am refusing to work."

He threatened to take me to "the Boards." I just answered "Let's go now then," and stepped out into the rain. I didn't care about "the Boards."

Ten minutes later I was banged up in the punishment block. It was only then I began to think, *Is this really happening to me? This is crazy! He probably will come back in ten minutes and let me out again.*

He didn't, I was banged up all weekend; it was the talk of the gaol.

Even other officers came in to see me; they couldn't believe it either; they told me the officer who charged me for refusing to work was a rookie— that is, he was only in the job about a week and I was his first charge.

It was monday before I knew the Governor would come to see me and, sure enough, my door opened and in he walked. This was the wing Governor whom I'd asked to have the Baptism service in the bath-house a few months before.

"What's this I hear Hamilton, that you refused to work? Tell me it's not true."

"I am afraid, sir, it is," I replied.

I went on to tell him the whole story, but of course the officer had told a different story: he just forgot to say about it raining at the time!

The Governor then said to me "I suppose the Devil made you do this, Hamilton?"

I answered "No sir, the Devil had nothing to do with this, it was just between your officer and me and I didn't like his attitude."

He looked at me and smiled slightly, "And I don't like your behaviour; your parole is cancelled."

I was stunned—I wasn't expecting this, no parole. I had been reading a Bible that was in the cell when the Governor walked in, I had my finger in it still to keep my place as I sat down after he had gone. I immediately began to pray, "God you can overrule this man, and get me my parole back for Monday." I looked down at the Bible and the last four words on the page said "NO I WILL NOT." I could not believe it ! You can't even argue with that! Well you can, but it does you no good: God and I argue all the time, and he always wins!

Two days later I was reading my Bible, while waiting for my door to open to let me out for church. Although on punishment we still got out for church. But I knew I would be separated from everybody else, I'd be up in the balcony sitting with an officer.

While sitting reading in Matthew 7 about the wise and foolish builders, I noticed that the trials were exactly the same for both guys (verses 25 &27), regardless of the one being a Christian. So I said to the Lord "That's not fair, the foolish guy, he deserves it, but not the wise guy. Why should he have the trials?" I believe God spoke into my mind and said "Why not? Just because he believes in the Lord, do you think then he should walk around with the sun shining on him while it rains on everyone else?"

The truth is we ALL go through the trials and storms of life, but for the Christian the outcome is different because he knows the Bible says that "All things work together for good to them that love God" (Romans 8:28). Sometimes we cannot see how this is possible, but the Bible says "We KNOW": we have God's assurance, as we are standing on the rock. God is with us in every trial. Tough times don't last, but tough people do!

This revelation blessed me, next thing I knew my door opened, and was locked back. "Combined Service" the officer shouted as he passed by to open the next cell.

I walked behind the officer and climbed the spiral staircase which led to the prison chapel. I was sitting alone, back at the door, two officers were standing talking together. I could see all the boys sitting down below me, everyone was talking and shouting across the aisle, the Chaplain hadn't come out of the vestry yet to start the service. I wondered who would be taking the service this morning.

It was the Rev. Jackson Buick, the new Presbyterian minister who had replaced Bill Vance. He was a small man in stature but what he lacked in height, he made up for in courage and stamina. He had a heart like a lion. But that first morning as he reached the lectern and stood up on it, he could barely see over the top. He stood up on his toes and looked over the top and said, "I don't know if I am to preach over this or under it." The place erupted with laughter. The boys liked his humour. I enjoyed his preaching a lot. We soon became good friends.

I was sitting up in the balcony waiting to hear what his sermon would be this particular morning. He opened the Bible and the boys all quieted down. A few moments later he began to read, "The wise man builds his house upon the rock." I just felt a surge within me and before I could stop myself I yelled at the top of my voice "Hallelujah" the two officers beside me almost jumped out of their skin! Everyone sitting down below turned around and looked up at me. I put my fist up in the air and shouted Hallelujah again. One of the guys shouted out "Packie is crazy." Jackson looked up at me gave me a smile and carried on with his reading. I was thrilled and knew God wanted me to remember what he had shown me earlier that morning.

CHAPTER SEVENTEEN

STEPPING OUT IN FAITH

I had found out an old mate of mine outside had also been converted. He started to visit me occasionally. Neither of us could have ever imagined then we would later become in-laws. Billy Smith was Sharon's brother. Often I would put his wife's name on the visit pass. On one occasion, she couldn't make it and Sharon came up instead. This was the first time I had seen her in years.

I knew that she had been living with her brother for the past few years, since the break-up of her first marriage. I enjoyed it when she came up to visit me. But I never thought any further than that. I didn't think she would be interested in forming a relationship with me. I knew years ago she had a real crush on me, but she was just a young teenager then.

I was glad it was in my last six months when I started to fall in love with Sharon, I enjoyed being around her: all we would talk about on our visits was the Lord. I decided if I were to marry again, it would be a woman who had these same qualities about her.

I honestly never thought before about marrying Sharon—simply because I'd known her for so long.

During my second parole I went to visit her brother. Later on that night he decided to go on to bed and handed us each a cup of tea before he went upstairs. This was the first time I had ever been alone with her. Previously, we were always in the company of others. We sat and talked into the early hours of the morning. We drank so much tea we eventually had to go out looking to buy some milk at about six o'clock in the morning. By that time I was hooked on her!

I went back into prison with her photograph in my Bible. I was showing all my mates her picture, "See my girlfriend guys." When they looked at the photo they said "but that's the girl who has been coming up to visit you regularly; was she not your girl then?" I said "No, we were just good friends" they laughed, "Sure, just good friends was that all?" They didn't believe me.

I was lying in bed one night looking at some photographs of Sharon and her little daughter Louise. As I was looking at Louise's photograph I had another experience from the Lord: suddenly it was as if gallons of love was poured into my heart for this little girl, and I began to cry for her. I fell in love with her too. She was a special gift because God had given her to me also. She became my daughter that night and so I wrote a letter and told her so.

Seven months after my release Sharon and I got married. Because I was in love, it made those last few months seem to go slow.

By fasting and prayer I learned to know when God was speaking to me, I found the Bible to be alive to me. Truly it is a living Word! No matter what I needed the answer to, somehow God would show me during these times what His will and purpose was. I developed such a hunger for the word of God, even the chaplain told me I was reading it too much! I have been known to sit up all night and read—I still do it—there are days I do nothing else but sit and read for hours on end, maybe six hours at a time. I never sit down to read without a pen, rule and paper. I like to underline my Bible as I read it, many verses in my Bible are dated when God has spoken through them to me at that particular time.

One time while in the Spirit, God spoke and told me that a preacher was coming into speak at a service and that he would have a special word for me. I was told a few days later that a team from the Christian Renewal Centre from Rostrevor were coming to minister to us. I was excited about this! because I knew something was going to happen.

The Christian Renewal Centre was founded by Cecil and Myrtle Kerr in 1974 as an oasis of peace amidst the violence of Northern Ireland, a community where Protestants and Catholics come together in reconciliation. It's a place I've visited many times since coming out of prison, Rostrevor is situated on the border between Ulster and the Irish Republic and to me it symbolises the white flag of neutrality between the orange and the green.

I remember that Sunday well. The Rev. Cecil Kerr lead a team as they ministered in various ways with the use of drama and song. Then Cecil shared a message with us; as he spoke I was listening really attentively, in case I missed what God wanted to say. Well the service ended, and still I hadn't got anything out of it. Even if he sneezed I wrote it down! Man, was I disappointed—until Cecil did something really strange. By this time men were walking out of the chapel. Cecil shouted to the officer, "Hold it one moment! ask those men to come back in again, I feel God is prompting me to say something to someone in here. It seems the unlikeliest of places but God is speaking to a man here today whom he will use as an evangelist outside. He may not be another Billy Graham, but he will win many people to Jesus Christ."

I couldn't believe it. I almost started to cry; I had to really brace myself to stop me from doing so. Somebody looked over at me and shouted, "That's Packie he's talking about!" I was hoping for a word but nothing so explicit as this, I couldn't wait to get out of there.

Back in my cell a few moments later, another Christian friend came running in, "That was powerful, Packie!" he said. I couldn't even answer. All I did was sit on the bed and only then did I start to cry. This is one of the greatest experiences of my Christian walk, even now when I look back and see that prophecy fulfilled, 14 years later! Since coming out of prison, I have seen thousands of souls saved, in many different countries. God has provided for me in miraculous ways and has given me the opportunity to preach His Gospel on Satellite television and to visit many cities and towns all over Europe, from the borders of the Ukraine in the East to Los Angeles in the West of the United States of America.

What a mighty God we serve!!

I will never forget hearing the words "HAMILTON TIME SERVED" as I walked across the yard for the last time. I had watched others for years step out to freedom, and now it was my turn. Some officers shouted farewell to me, I smiled and waved. It was with a mixture of emotions, I was leaving some guys in there I had come to love as brothers, and yet I was walking out to a new life.

Packie Hamilton the Terrorist was dead it was now Packie Hamilton the Evangelist going out the gate. I knew I would never do time again. I was wondering what would happen in my life now. I didn't know what it was like to live as a Christian outside.

Those first few months were really hard; at times I thought, *It would be easier in gaol*. Getting used to carrying money around, able to open and close doors for myself, learning to eat of a plate instead of a steel tray, turning lights on and off for myself: all those little things people take for granted. Even finding out I could have free medical prescriptions: I naturally assumed I had to pay for them, which I did. I was not long going back to the chemist and asking if I could have my money back as I didn't know about unemployment benefits.

Then there was the Organisation too. I knew I had to face them. Sure enough, I wasn't long out when I had a visit from one of them. The UVF Commanders wanted to see me. I was told to be at a bar in Belfast on such and such a date. I was told "Make sure you're there—we don't want to have to go looking for you." I was not going to try and hide or take off somewhere. "I'll be there, tell them," I told him.

I didn't tell any of my family, apart from my brother. He said he would come with me. "You can't go alone," he said. I told him, "I will not be alone, God will be there with me so I am not worried." He was afraid for me.

I had thought about this many times before in gaol. Now this was it. I thought of what I would say to them. I knew one man already from my old UVF team who had been shot dead. He had become a Christian and tried to leave.

I was leaving, no matter what. My mind was already made up. I was finished with it all. If they shoot me I will be in glory. I thought about that. I had no fear, none at all.

Friday arrived. We set off; my Brother was telling me if you're not out in such an such a time I will call the police. It was obvious who was the more afraid. Naturally, because at that time he was not yet converted.

Today he is also a minister of the gospel—Praise God! Also my own story is far from finished. My conversion in prison reads only as an introduction to what God continues to do in my life up until now. If the truth be told, what has happened to me since my release, God leading me on to greater heights and new fresh personal experiences of his wonderful grace and abounding love, far excels the story of my life prior to my conversion. Of course my salvation is something I will never cease to be thankful for. Over the years I've found out that Salvation is truly the greatest miracle of all. But there is an onward journey, a pressing on to know Him more. If God grants me grace, I plan to set all this down in a sequel volume.

As we drove along I thought back to the time I first came to this bar to join Them. I had really believed it was a cause worth dying for, but Jesus had given me a new cause, a cause worth *living* for.

I decided the gospel of Jesus Christ is the only cause worth dying for. I was ready to die if that was the case. I could do nothing else. There was no other choice for me. I saw it quite clear cut, I had given my life to Christ, I could not deny him.

We stopped across the road from the bar. I said to my brother, "Here goes," and jumped and ran across the road through the door into the bar........But that's another story.

POSTSCRIPT

I feel it's only proper to add a point here which is worth noting: The prison system today is no longer the same as it was in my day. It has completely changed in Northern Ireland, over the past ten years since my release. There has been much reform, neither is it all for the good. I visit some prisoners who were in with me and who are still there—one guy is into his 18th year. He has told me it is altogether different. You do not have to call the guards, "Sir". There is no more having to work during the day, there are no more lock-ups during the day. You are allowed to go over to other wings to visit. The guards don't even come down the wings anymore, they just call out your name and wait for you. Nowadays it's all on first name terms for guards and prisoners alike. You can have television in your cell, three or four can lock-up in the big cell together and watch movies all night long.

When my friend told me all this I answered, "Man you have it easy now. That's not doing time."

I was shocked by his answer, "The truth is Packie, it's harder now than it was in your time. Then we made the most of our free time, because we were working during the day. Time went by a lot faster. Do you see now? It's worse, a lot of guys can't get their time in. Now there is more fighting amongst themselves. Before, in the old days if you had problems with a guard you would punch him, go to the punishment cell, a few guards would come in and beat you for 10 minutes and that was it. Nowadays it's five or six guys beating a guard, and not with their fists. They use the steel bars of the weights to attack them. A lot of this is because they are bored with nothing to do.

"A lot of guys are into drugs now. Remember in the old days we made the home-brew with all the fruit? Not anymore. It's dope which is the thing now and it's increasing. Believe me, the old days were better."

Of course there are good points about it as well. For instance the visits are far better; not just tables beside each other like in the old days, they have more privacy now. Back then the visit lasted half an hour once a week, and many times you were lucky even to get that. Nowadays, a visit could last possibly two hours if things are not too busy.

Having said all that, prison is still prison regardless of privileges. It's the loss of freedom that cannot be replaced. Prison is always hard, regardless of how long the stay. It seems the longer one does the harder it is to get it out of one's mind. It can take some men years to learn to cope with life on the outside again. Others remain institutionalised.

I've come to realise prison leaves scars, some of which remain tender for a long time. Others, it seems, never really heal properly.

CONCLUSION

A CAUSE WORTH LIVING FOR

What is the point of life? It's hardly a new question: it's as old, in fact, as the story of Adam and Eve. Everyone knows how Eve and then Adam decided to disobey God and eat from the Tree of the Knowledge of Good and Evil. The point is not just that Adam and Eve disobeyed. The profound thing is that they chose *the knowledge of good and evil*: not evil alone —note—but a mixture of the two. Can we find fulfilment in doing only as we are told or do we *need* the excitement of rebellion?

The suspicion is that we do, because when we observe successful people, we rarely see 'goody-goodies': what we generally see is people who dared to be different in a way that was attractive to others—and usually there's a mixture of good and evil. It's even one of the stock themes of Hollywood to stage a battle against evil where the baddies run rings round the head of police, who plays by the rules. Only our hero (who is undisciplined at work, and 'into' wine, women and song) can win—by disobeying the rules. Even in the Bible, we see winners like David or Jacob playing by their own rules . . .

Are you getting the point about the knowledge of good and evil? When I joined up as a terrorist I was deciding for myself the boundary of good and evil. Other people make their choices in different areas: this taxpayer decides how much tax it is 'reasonable' to pay; that student concludes that drugs are a legitimate form of recreation . . . We all have the freedom to make such choices but it's not in our power to decree either that these things will satisfy our longings or that they will go unpunished.

Further, the knowledge of good and evil often incorporates the privilege of deciding whom to be good to and whom to be bad to; that was very strong, obviously, in my own Loyalist circle. But it is not very different when a teenager is popular with his peers and nasty to his parents; or when a businessman is scrupulous with his clients and oppressive to his workers.

This mixture of good and evil is also what makes us uneasy about religious fanatics: they can suddenly change from being near perfect into persecutors of the worst kind. Did you know that the great apostle Paul branded himself the worst sinner of all for this very reason, because he thought it right to put to death the first Christians?

Don't we all want both to be approved and to do our own thing? Christians are not sinless, they just sin less—and claim to follow a 'cause' whose leader *is* perfect. Do we need a 'cause' to find meaning in life? Well, it is often 'convenient' to pick some enemies as well as friends: having an enemy allows us to break rules, to be strong and authoritarian ... But we don't in fact have to be aggressive to have enemies. My own insight into this is that becoming known as a Christian is tough—we have an enemy who is all the more powerful in that he is unseen and spiritual. It was tough to be a terrorist, but it is tough to be Christian too: plenty of people avoid becoming Christians because they are scared of the crowd. For, deep down, the crowd approves of Adam and Eve: not all good, not all bad—just the winning mixture.

A relentless spirit of boredom and frustration is now gripping our society. Stand outside any school on Monday morning and watch the kids dragging themselves into their classrooms. Their faces say it all, they seem to resent "having to go" to school. They count the minutes until lunch time. For the majority they seem to leave as bored as they came. One sixteen-year-old girl told me "Life's a bore, school's a bore, I can't imagine going a whole week-end without a smoke of dope, it's the only thing that helps break-up the monotony, and even then you still feel down; Why is it nothing I do makes me happy?"

Few can explain why they feel so down and empty. Surely, the reason is that God loves us too much to allow us to enjoy our ill-gotten gains for ever – the truth is these things can never truly satisfy. More positively, God created mankind as spiritual beings; we are made up of spirit, soul and body. We cater for the flesh and neglect the spirit, when we were made to have a relationship with God. No human being can discover his or her full potential outside of this relationship.

And this leads me to the ultimate question: what do you think of Jesus Christ? The Jewish leaders saw him as one who used unexplained psychic powers to convince ordinary people of a 'preposterous' claim to be God's anointed saviour—Messiah. The Roman governor thought of him as a harmless itinerant preacher. But those closest to Jesus believed that he controls the very keys of the Kingdom of Heaven. The Bible says;

> For just as the Father raises the dead and gives them life, even so the Son gives life to whom he is pleased to give it. (John 5:21).

This in effect ups the stakes, because it means that our view of Christ affects our eternal destiny. Indeed, the Bible actually spells out "He who does not believe stands condemned already" (John 3:18). But Jesus certainly does not want to condemn anyone:

> Jesus said, 'I am the light of the world; Whoever follows me will never walk in darkness, but will have the light of life' (John 8:12).

> Jesus said, 'The thief comes only to steal kill and to destroy; I have come that they may have life and have it to the full' (John 10:10).

> Jesus said, 'I am the resurrection and the life: He who believes me will live, even though he dies' (John 11:25).

> Jesus said, 'I am the way, the truth, and the life no one comes to the Father except through me' (John 14:6).

> But these things are written that you may believe that Jesus is the Christ, the Son of God, and that by believing you may have life in his name   (John 20:31).

Christ does not offer a new start in life, but rather a new life to start! Think about that!

> Therefore, if anyone is in Christ, he is a new creation, the old has gone, the new has come (2 Corinthians 5:17).

Are you tired of all the heartache, the unfulfilled longings, the loneliness and despair? Are you through with the endless tit-for-tat of trying to defend your own honour? Do you really want to change your lifestyle? If so, do something about it—right now! There is nothing to lose, but everything to gain. Believe Jesus when he says, 'Whoever comes to me I will never drive away' (John 6:37).

Believe in Him and do as He asks, 'Come to me, all you who are weary and burdened, and I will give you rest' (Matthew 11: 38).

The testimony of millions, ever since the death and resurrection of Christ, is that through faith in Him they have discovered the true meaning of life. In simple childlike faith, they believed the words of Christ and were set free from their emptiness and despair. Friend, taken from the pages of God's Holy Word are the simple steps to finding reality through Jesus Christ. It is up to you to believe and act on what you see and hear.

1. Believe Christ is your friend and that He cares about you (1 Peter 5:7).

2. Call upon Him for help—right now (Matthew 11:28-30).

3. Believe Him to save you from your sin, depression, and fear (Romans 10:9).

4. Confess Him publicly as your Lord and Saviour (1 John 5:24).

5. Believe He will cleanse you and make you a new person (2 Cor 5:17).

6. Simply trust Him with childlike faith (Ephesians 2:8).

PRAY THIS SIMPLE PRAYER, IN FAITH:

Lord Jesus Christ, with my mouth I confess my sins, my selfishness, in living my own way and not your way. Please forgive me; wipe my slate clean and give me a new life to begin. I renounce the Devil and all his ways and here and now I receive Christ as Lord of my Life. Fill me with your Holy Spirit, give me a hunger to read the Living Word of God and teach me how to pray. Thank you Lord for answering my prayer, in Jesus Name I pray. Amen.

If you have trusted Christ through reading this book, please tell another Christian. And we will be greatly encouraged if you also write and tell us!

THE ARK
Life Challenge Manchester
1 Justin Close
Chorlton on Medlock
Manchester M13 9WX   TEL: 0161 2732 532